WORKING ACROSS CULTURES

Applications and Exercises

Martin J. Gannon

 Sage Publications, Inc.
International Educational and Professional Publisher
Thousand Oaks ▪ London ▪ New Delhi

For information:

Sage Publications, Inc.
2455 Teller Road
Thousand Oaks, California 91320
E-mail: order@sagepub.com

Sage Publications Ltd.
6 Bonhill Street
London EC2A 4PU
United Kingdom

Sage Publications India Pvt. Ltd.
M-32 Market
Greater Kailash I
New Delhi 110 048 India

Printed in the United States of America

Library of Congress Cataloging-in-Publication Data

Gannon, Martin J.
    Working across cultures: Applications and exercises / by Martin J. Gannon.
        p. cm.
Includes bibliographical references and index.
    ISBN 0-7619-1338-6
    1. Culture—Research. 2. Culture—Study and teaching. 3. Cross-cultural orientation. 4. Social problems. I. Title.
    HM623 .G36 2000
    306´.07—dc21

                                                    00-008947

01 02 03 10 9 8 7 6 5 4 3 2 1

Acquiring Editor:	Marquita Flemming
Editorial Assistant:	MaryAnn Vail
Production Editor:	Diana E. Axelsen
Editorial Assistant:	Cindy Bear
Typesetter/Designer:	Lynn Miyata/Rebecca Evans
Indexer:	Mary Mortensen
Cover Designer:	Michelle Lee

Contents

Preface: Using This Book

The underlying premise of this book is that cross-cultural understanding is maximally achieved through the active involvement of the student or trainee in the learning process, but that this involvement must be based on a thorough grounding in theory. Even a very knowledgeable instructor lecturing on culture always faces the implicit—and sometimes not so implicit—assumption among trainees and students that they know as much as, if not more than, the instructor. The use of exercises forces students, trainees, and instructor to grapple with the complexity of culture in an active manner.

Furthermore, as the subtitle of the book indicates, it is not sufficient to be actively involved in exercises; the instructor must also show how cultural concepts and exercises apply in real-world situations. This is an applications book that presents a wide diversity of learning experiences in different formats, such as completing self-administered questionnaires, undertaking culture-focused interviews, debating pros and cons on a particular issue, analyzing short case studies, creating an advertising campaign, and redesigning work groups through using cultural knowledge.

Most exercise books include 20 to 30 exercises that the authors explain in detail, identifying the goals of each exercise, the amount of time required, and so on. In contrast, this book includes a large number of exercises (71, plus Chapters 9 through 11) containing lecture materials, examples, and a wide variety of perspectives. I have found these examples and approaches to be enriching and helpful in the classroom, but each instructor can tailor each exercise to his or her needs, preferences, and time constraints. Also, I opted for a large and diverse number of exercises so that the instructor can review quickly for ideas and approaches that are personally appealing and can be implemented quickly with minimal effort. The instructor can either proceed sequentially through the book or examine the table of contents and select exercises that are personally appealing.

The exercises are based on 15 years of cross-cultural training of undergraduate and MBA students at the University of Maryland and several non-American universities in Europe and Asia. Also, the material has been class-tested in cross-cultural management training programs, including the IMPACT Certificate Program (International Management Program and Compliance Training) at Northrop-Grumman, Baltimore, Maryland, and the Senior Management Training Program at GEICO.

Students and trainees are strongly encouraged to participate in discussions and group meetings in many of these exercises. I also recommend the use of the "think-pair-share" method, whereby the instructor presents a question to be answered but allows the class 1 minute of silence, following which each class member discusses ideas with another class member sitting in an adjacent chair. There is then a general class discussion, which allows class members to take ownership of the learning process, thereby enhancing it.

This book can be used either independently or to accompany *Understanding Global Cultures* (Gannon and Associates, 2001). All of the exercises relate to the concept of cultural metaphors, that is, a unique or distinctive phenomenon, activity, or institution with which members of an ethnic or national culture closely identify, which they understand, and which symbolizes their shared but frequently unconsciously held values, such as the Chinese family altar or the Swedish stuga. Triandis (in press) feels that this is the most interesting aspect of culture; similarly, Brislin (1993) believes that culture allows the individual to automatically fill in the blanks when behavior is required; and Hofstede (1991) defines culture as mental programming, or the software of the mind. It is this feature of culture that is not only very interesting but also problematic, because the instructor must involve trainees and students in the learning process to move such shared values from the background into the foreground.

Chapter 1 provides some initial exercises on cross-cultural differences; the focus in Chapters 2 and 3 is on developing exercises for well-known cross-cultural dimensions such as individualism-collectivism, power distance, time, and space. Chapter 4 presents several exercises on cultural metaphors that are designed to supplement the use of cross-cultural dimensions, whereas Chapter 5 presents exercises involving a new typology of cultures based on the concepts of processes, outcomes, and degree of emotional expressiveness. Chapter 6 looks at the area of sociolinguistics, or the interaction between language and society, and Chapter 7 treats some additional behaviors across cultures, including an exploration of the four basic types of human relations. Chapter 8 explores the issue of cross-cultural negotiating, and Chapters 9 and 10 take an in-depth look at the cultural metaphors for Germany and Japan. The book concludes by recommending training videos that can serve to enhance the learning process.

Michele Gelfand, Assistant Professor of Organizational and Cross-Cultural Psychology at the University of Maryland, authored Exercise 4.8, debating the merits of cultural metaphors, and Exercise 4.19, on organization design and work groups. I edited these exercises for this book with her permission. Also, I have used other sources, as noted, in developing exercises, but I centered these exercises around the concept of cultural metaphors.

I would like to thank two Maryland MBAs, Claire Boehmler and Mark Davis, for their research assistance. As usual, the Robert H. Smith School of Business at the University of Maryland at College Park has provided a congenial and intellectually stimulating environment in which to work, for which I am most appreciative. Finally, if the reader comes across any errors or ways of improving the book, I would be grateful if he or she would bring them to my attention (mgannon@rhsmith. umd.edu).

CHAPTER 1

Understanding Cross-Cultural Differences

Many individuals do not consider cultural differences or culture to be important. They believe that individuals tend to be similar across cultures. In fact, however, culture has a major impact on the effectiveness of teams. Teams comprised of all members from a single culture tend to be of average effectiveness. In contrast, multicultural teams have the potential to be the most effective and productive teams in organizations, but they also can be the least productive. Just as there are cultural paradoxes, so too there is the paradox of multicultural team effectiveness.

Figure 1.1 shows the relative productivity of a series of 800 four- to six-member teams as observed by Dr. Carol Kovach at UCLA (see Adler, 1997).

This figure provides some important insights. First, it is clear that there is a wide disparity in the effectiveness of multicultural teams, which suggests that certain factors in cross-cultural interactions and communication either facilitate or hinder the effectiveness of such teams. The figure also leads us to believe that diversity among team members is one quality that at least has the potential to increase effectiveness, whereas single-culture teams are limited in their ability to achieve high effectiveness.

EXERCISE 1.1 **Culture and Group Effectiveness**

This opening exercise and other ones in the early chapters address the importance of culture. Exercise 1.1 encourages students to explore reasons why there is a dis-

FIGURE 1.1. Single-Culture Groups, Cross-Cultural Groups, and Group Effectiveness

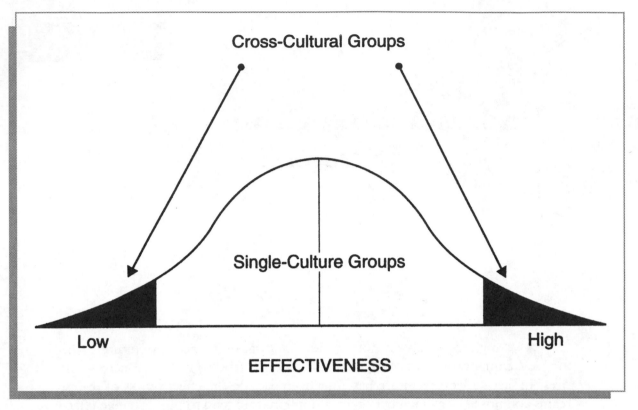

NOTE: See Adler (1997) and Cox (1993).

parity between the group effectiveness of cross-cultural and single-culture groups within organizations and to examine the major strengths and weaknesses of these two different types of groups. The exercise involves the use of the think-pair-share method, which has three stages:

1. Students think silently for 1 minute about a topic or question posed by the instructor.

2. Each student then discusses his or her thoughts with the student sitting next to him or her.

3. There is a class discussion of the topic.

■ COMMENTS

The instructor may want to point out that any minority group member in a team or group primarily composed of one type (e.g., a male in an all-female group) is treated as a token and not assumed to be any different in terms of values and behaviors until minority representation reaches 20% (see Cox, 1993). At or above that point, the group members realize that they no longer constitute a single-culture group. The group then tends to follow the traditional model of group dynamics:

- *Form or Reform:* The group members reevaluate each other and reorient themselves to the situation.

- *Storm:* In this stage, group members begin to engage in conflict with one another.

- *Norm:* During this stage, the group agrees on certain norms or rules governing behavior in the group.

- *Perform:* The group finally settles down to complete the assigned task.

The instructor can emphasize that it is critical to address conflicting values and attitudes directly and openly. Otherwise, effective norms or rules cannot be implemented, and low performance will result.

The instructor may also want to compare the well-known "trained incapacity" of functional specialists and single-culture groups. For example, marketing specialists tend to see the world primarily from the perspective of marketing. In a classic study that has been repeated several times, Simon and Dearborn (1958) asked managers from different functional backgrounds to identify the major issue in a business case study. The finance managers identified finance as the major issue, the human resource specialists focused on difficulties between individuals and groups, and so on.

Finally, the instructor may want to point out that creativity and effectiveness tend to be enhanced when diversity of all types is present. For example, Smith, Grimm, and Gannon (1992) showed that diversity in the composition of top management teams as measured by different types of functional backgrounds and education is related to organizational performance.

EXERCISE 1.2　　Culture and the Manager's Role

For this exercise, trainees or students should look at Figure 1.2. Using a think-pair-share approach, ask the trainees or students to discuss their thoughts as to why culture may influence the percentage of managers in each nation who agreed with the following statement: "It is important for managers to have at hand precise answers to most of the questions that their subordinates may raise about their work."

COMMENTS

National culture appears to influence not only team effectiveness in an organization but also managerial style, beliefs, and actions. As Figure 1.2 shows, the managers' cultural background affects how comfortable they are in working without

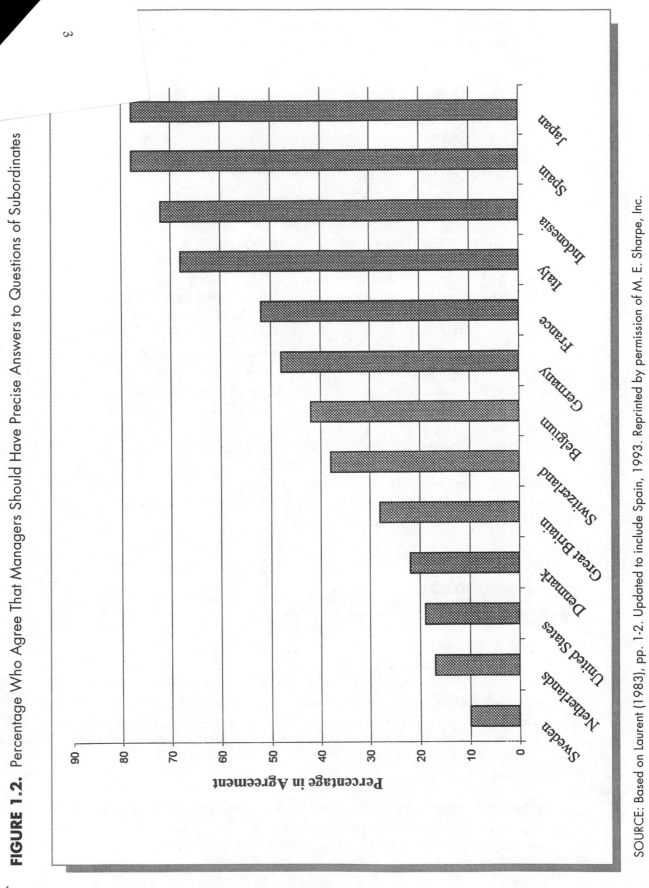

FIGURE 1.2. Percentage Who Agree That Managers Should Have Precise Answers to Questions of Subordinates

SOURCE: Based on Laurent (1983), pp. 1-2. Updated to include Spain, 1993. Reprinted by permission of M. E. Sharpe, Inc.

specific job knowledge about subordinate tasks. This graph can be tied to results from Hofstede's (1980) analysis of uncertainty avoidance or the acceptance of risk. One way to avoid uncertainty is to try to be an expert in all aspects of the work of subordinates. According to Hofstede's study, Japan ranks first among 53 national cultures on uncertainty avoidance. Thus, it is not surprising that managers from Japan were more likely than American managers to agree with the statement in Figure 1.2.

In sum, Figure 1.2 highlights that there are contrasting views as to whether a manager in an organization is supposed to be an expert or a delegator based on cultural differences. So, when organizations have managers and staff from different cultures, potential conflicts may arise if they are not sensitive to the inherent differences in expectations based on culture. Ideas about organizational structure vary across culture as well in a similar manner. That is, individuals from some nations tend to see an organization as much more hierarchical than do individuals from other nations (see Trompenaars & Hampden-Turner, 1998). The instructor can even draw two or three organizational structures on the board with different numbers of levels (e.g., 3, 5, and 9) and ask the students or trainees to identify the organizational structure that is most appropriate in their home nations, and why this is so.

EXERCISE 1.3   Preconceived Influences

Another example of how preconditioning can influence a person's behavior comes from the famous picture of the young/old lady. This is a classic exercise that has been popular for decades. The instructor should complete the exercise and then lead a discussion of the manner in which culture preconditions us, even though we are not conscious of this fact.

The instructor should split the classroom into two halves. He or she should ask those on one side of the room to close their eyes and then show those on the other side a sketch of an obviously young woman (see Figure 1.3).

The drawing of the woman is from the side, and all of the features are drawn in a quick and nondetailed manner. The instructor then repeats the process with the other half of the room, but this drawing is of an old woman, and her features are similarly nondetailed (see Figure 1.4). As an alternative to using an overhead, the instructor can distribute copies of the three drawings.

Once all of the students have looked at their drawings for a few seconds, the instructor then puts up an overhead drawing of a woman (see Figure 1.5).

This drawing is similar to both of the earlier drawings, and the sketch is made so that the features are not very detailed. After a moment, the instructor should ask the students, "What do you see?"

FIGURE 1.3.

FIGURE 1.4.

FIGURE 1.5.

What do you see?

■ **COMMENTS**

It is at this moment that the exercise becomes interesting. Typically, half of the class members believe that they are looking at a drawing of a young woman, and half feel that they are seeing an old woman. Even though the students are all in one room and looking at the same image, they are seeing two different pictures. Sometimes, the students in one half of the class will attempt to convince the others that the picture does not depict what they believe it to show. Eventually, each side of the class will begin to see the outline of the other woman, and begin to understand the optical illusion they have experienced. But even with a subsequent glance, some members of the class will probably see only the figure that they were influenced to see at first. Then, they will gradually see how both figures are in the same drawing.

This experience is similar to the effect that culture has on the way people interpret things. It gives clear evidence that two people can be looking at the same thing and see something quite different. And they can both be correct! Just as with the picture, very few people interpret things without relying on their cultural preconditioning. It is rare that a person from the first group would have thought that the drawing was of an older woman at first glance. That is because they believed that they were supposed to be seeing a young woman, and so they did.

Because the composite picture was drawn in a nondetailed manner, we had to fill in the blanks ourselves. Those who had just seen a picture of the young woman filled in the sketch with that information, and those who saw the old woman acted similarly, seeing only the old woman. Looking at the composite picture from a frame of reference other than your basic one is not common, and it is difficult. It is similar to how culture shapes our perceptions and behavior. As with cultural influences, when there is ambiguity in a situation, we rely upon automatic responses. Brislin (1993) indicates that culture allows us to fill in the blanks. It is hoped that as cross-cultural experiences and sophistication increase, we can fill in these blanks in a more encompassing and mature fashion.

EXERCISE 1.4	Language and Perception

The instructor may want to follow up this discussion by asking the students to count, within 20 seconds, the number of Fs in Figure 1.6.

Individuals whose primary language is English tend to see fewer Fs than do others. The instructor can ask for a show of hands indicating how many have seen one, two, three, four, five, or six Fs. The point is that culture conditions us to focus on some areas and not others.

The instructor may note that a bilingual person driving in an area where signs are posted in both languages tends to read the signs using only one language and frequently does not even notice the use of the second language. He might ask if anyone in the group has had this experience, and how it felt.

FIGURE 1.6. Please count the number of Fs (20-second limit).

FINISHED FILES ARE

THE RESULT OF YEARS

OF SCIENTIFIC STUDY

COMBINED WITH THE

EXPERIENCE OF YEARS

EXERCISE 1.5   Metaphors for Culture

Begin this exercise by talking about metaphors of organization. For example, the dominant metaphor until about 1960—and it is popular even today—is that an organization is a machine. If one part breaks down, the entire machine breaks down. Hence, many organizations have tall or multilevel hierarchies in which decision making is centralized at the top and everyone is supervised closely to avoid mistakes. Using think-pair-share, ask students to identify their metaphors of culture itself. The machine is excluded as a choice. Write metaphors on the blackboard or overhead and lead a discussion. Some metaphors that frequently come up are the following:

- Computer
- A tree
- The brain
- A whale
- The gene pool
- A rainbow
- A prism
- A school
- A skyscraper
- A body or organism
- A filter

You may want to point out that both Geert Hofstede (1991) and Glen Fisher (1988) use the computer as a metaphor for culture. In Hofstede's intriguing phrase, culture represents the software of the mind.

■ COMMENTS

The variations in solutions to creating a metaphor for culture are related to the complexity of the concept. There are, in fact, many ways of looking at culture. Schein (1985) indicates that culture has multiple levels. The first level in Schein's model includes the visible things that a culture produces. These are the artifacts and products of a culture that we can see, hear, or feel. The next level is only partially observable and includes values and ideals that members of the culture value and tend to use to mold their behavior. These values are often unspoken, and they can create conflict when either members of the culture or outsiders violate them. Schein's last or deepest level is what he terms a culture's assumptions. For example, some cultures assume that humans are intrinsically evil, whereas other cultures believe that humans are intrinsically good. Other cultures fall somewhere in the middle of these extreme points.

EXERCISE 1.6	Cultural Identity

This is an exercise that is to be completed individually, and then it can be shared with the class. Have each student draw a circle on a piece of paper. Then, in the circle, have students construct pie charts that describes their identity as they see it in terms of the groups with which they are associated and that they consider to be important. The degree of importance of each group is represented by the magnitude of each slice. No further instructions should be given. The students should have about 5 minutes to complete the exercise. Then, ask individuals if they would mind describing their circles. Hold each sheet of paper so that class members can see the drawing when the individual speaks. Do not be judgmental, but you can ask for clarifications. Then, show Figure 1.7 as an example. Indicate that other examples are frequently less complex (e.g., there may be only three categories, and being Christian may take up 60% of the chart).

FIGURE 1.7. Cultural Identity of an MBA Student

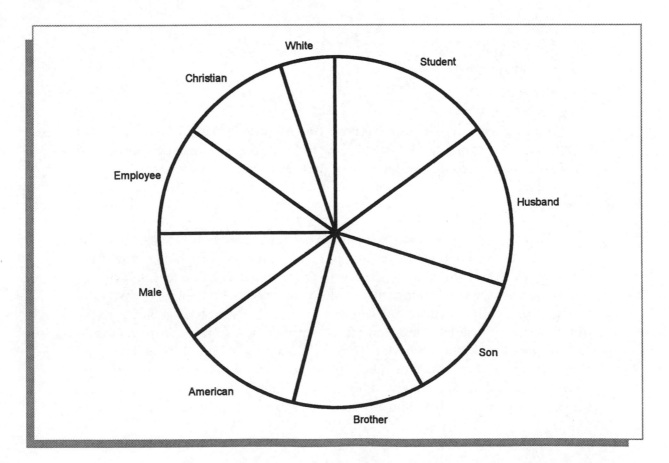

■ COMMENTS

There are no correct or incorrect answers in this exercise. What is important is to get an idea of how differently people categorize themselves with regards to the groups with which they identify. It is also interesting to see how much emphasis an individual gives to a specific group. For example, a highly individualistic person may identify with groups in which they have been very successful—such as a work group or professional organization—rather than with family, friends, and community.

The instructor may want to point out that individualistic Americans tend to respond differently from the Japanese to the simple cocktail party question: What do you do? Americans tend to respond initially in terms of occupation and then identify the company in which they work. The more collectivistic Japanese reverse this order. The instructor may even ask the students or trainees to answer this question *before* describing the standard American and Japanese responses.

EXERCISE 1.7 — Nationalism, Ethnicity, and Globalization

Create an overhead with the eight questions in Figure 1.8. You should use this questionnaire to generate discussion on national identity and globalization. Point out that in 1970, less than 5% of the U.S. gross domestic product was generated by international trade, but that by 1996, the percentage was almost 25, or $1.6 trillion. After students have thought about their answers, have them discuss these answers with the person next to them (think, pair, share). If time permits, tabulate and show the responses on the blackboard or overhead.

■ COMMENTS

This exercise can be related to the emergence of the European Community (EC). Several nations, such as England and Finland, have resisted this concept for decades, but it is now a reality. However, although each nation has retained fiscal authority, there is now a unified monetary authority or single interest rate for all involved nations. This has been termed "the great experiment," because it has been tried several times in the past and has failed.

The instructor may want to ask why. The short answer is that, when a nation is experiencing difficulties such as excessive unemployment, its politicians are tempted to solve the problems by manipulating the interest rate.

Furthermore, there have been several surveys asking citizens whether they identify primarily with Europe or their respective nations. Percentages have varied over time, but more Germans proportionately identify primarily with Europe than does any other nationality. Germany and France have been the leaders in the formation of the EC.

FIGURE 1.8. National/Ethnicity/Globalization Questionnaire

1. When you hear the word *nationalism,* how do you feel?
   (negative, neutral, positive)

2. When you hear the word *globalization,* how do you feel?
   (negative, neutral, positive)

3. Are the two concepts in opposition to one another, parallel to one another,
   or supplementary/complementary?

4. Name a country or event that comes to mind when you hear the word *nationalism.*

5. Name a country or event that comes to mind when you hear the word *globalization.*

6. Is a nation an imagined political community?

7. Is nation an obsolete concept?

8. When you hear the name of an ethnic group to which you belong (e.g., Irish–
   American), how do you feel? (negative, neutral, positive)

For information on this topic, see Gannon (2001), particularly the readings and research translations devoted to whether the nation-state is becoming less important as globalization increases. The instructor may want to point to the EC as evidence supporting this view. However, as the readings and research translations show, the importance of the nation-state is still strong and possibly increasing because of the need to balance the complex and often conflicting desires specific to each nation. Also, as the research translation of Samuel Huntington's book (Gannon, in press) shows, ethnic groups based on religious and linguistic differences within nations are becoming more assertive. It is these groups that have been engaging disproportionately in wars within nations (e.g., the Roman Catholic Croatians, the Muslim Bosnians, and the Russian Orthodox Serbians in Yugoslavia).

CHAPTER 2

The Dimensions of Culture: Part I

Continuing with our applications and exercises on culture, we are now going to get more familiar with the concept of cultural dimensions. Anthropologists and psychologists have studied intensively the dimensions along which cultures can vary; today, we use these dimensions in business applications. The work we will emphasize in this chapter is that of Florence Kluckholn and Fred Strodtbeck (1961), and also of Edward T. Hall (Hall & Hall, 1990). In the next chapter, we will continue the discussion of cross-cultural dimensions.

Kluckholn and Strodtbeck measured cultural differences along six dimensions in a series of studies in small communities. They noted that each culture had a dominant orientation with regard to each of the six dimensions, although a subordinate orientation could coexist with it. For example, an ethnic group could be individualistic overall, but a significant number of its members might be collectivistic. Their list of questions appears in Table 2.1. They also noted that writers on culture have emphasized these six dimensions for several centuries.

Another anthropologist who worked in this area was Edward T. Hall. He studied cultural differences as well, with the majority of his work focused on communication patterns used within cultures. See Hall's dimensions in Table 2.2.

The exercises in this chapter will emphasize the learning of these dimensions and refinements of them. For additional information on this topic, see Chapter 1 in Gannon and Associates (2001).

TABLE 2.1: Kluckholn and Strodtbeck's Six Dimensions of Culture

1. What do members of a society assume about the nature of people—that is, are people good, bad, or a combination?

2. What do members of a society assume about the relationship between a person and nature—that is, should we live in harmony with nature or subjugate it?

3. What do members of a society assume about the relationship between people—that is, should a person act in an individual manner or consider the group before taking action?

4. What is the primary mode of activity in a given society? Is it "being"—accepting the status quo, enjoying the current situation, and going with the flow of things—or is it "doing"—changing things to make them better, setting specific goals, accomplishing them within specific schedules, and so forth?

5. What is the conception of space in a given society—that is, is space considered *private* in that meetings are held in private, people do not get too close to one another physically, and so on; or *public*, that is, having everyone participate in meetings and decision making, allowing emotions to be expressed publicly, and having people stand in close proximity to one another?

6. What is the society's dominant temporal orientation—past, present, or future?

TABLE 2.2: Hall's Dimensions of Culture as Related to Communication

1. SPACE, or the ways of communicating through specific handling of personal space

2. TIME, which is either *monochronic* (scheduling and completing one activity at a time) or *polychronic* (not distinguishing between activities and completing them simultaneously)

3. CONTEXT, or the amount of information that must be stated explicitly if a message or communication is to be successful. Low-context cultures are those in which individuals need a great amount of background or written and oral information before the communication can be effective. High-context cultures are those in which individuals are socialized heavily so that they do not need a great amount of written and oral information.

4. INFORMATION FLOW, which is the structure and speed of messages between individuals or organizations.

EXERCISE 2.1   Arrival Times for Different Activities

Using the think-pair-share method, have students answer the following questions:

In general, how early or late should you arrive for

1. a job interview?

2. the MBA orientation session before the start of the program?

3. a first date?

4. a party?

5. a dinner party?

6. your regular job?

■ COMMENTS

Note how answers may vary by circumstances. For example, individuals may tend to emphasize promptness for a job interview, but feel that arriving 2 hours after a party has begun is good form. Then, point out that different cultures will tend to respond somewhat differently. For example, some cultures in northern Europe, such as the Swedish culture, tend to emphasize arriving at a dinner party promptly, whereas some Latin American cultures are not concerned if guests arrive 15 or 20 minutes late.

Furthermore, the instructor can emphasize how the issue of time is related to politeness. For example, in some areas of Latin America and Africa, it is not polite to refuse a party or dinner invitation. However, it is acceptable to not show up! This is an indirect or high-context way of saying no.

EXERCISE 2.2   Time as Past, Present, and Future

A very involving short exercise concerning time uses the following instructions (Cottle, 1967).

Think of the past, present, and future as being the shape of circles. Please draw three circles on a sheet of paper representing the past, the present, and the future. Arrange these three circles in any way that best shows how you feel about the relationship of the past, present, and future. You may use different size circles. When you have finished, label each circle to show which is the past, which is the present, and which is the future.

■ COMMENTS

After the students or trainees have completed the exercise, the instructor should ask selected individuals if they will explain their drawings, which the instructor can hold up for all to see. As each person is speaking, the instructor can discuss the following ways of classifying time: linear versus nonlinear or cyclical; the past, present, and the future; and monochronic versus polychronic (see Table 2.3). A good question to ask is the following: How would a Buddhist draw the three circles? The answer is one circle, because Buddhism recognizes only one time in which the past, present, and future overlay (see below). The instructor may also want to talk about the difficulty of interaction and/or negotiation when a linear-focused individual and a Buddhist-focused individual communicate with one another. A similar nonlinear view of time is expressed in the Mayan belief of a 260-year repeating cycle. Nonlinear orientations to time tend to be dominant in large parts of Asia, Africa, and Latin America.

Furthermore, different cultures vary in their preferred orientation to time. Past-oriented cultures idealize their ancestors and achievements of the past. Present-focused cultures are typically concerned with present survival and subsistence. Future-thinking cultures are those whose members believe that they can influence the future through their achievements. At this point, the instructor might ask, What is the dominant time orientation in the United States? Typically, students or trainees will choose the present and/or the future. The instructor can point out that different ethnic subgroups may choose differently.

An interesting study highlighting cultural orientations toward time was completed by Trompenaars and Hampden-Turner (1998). He asked 15,000 managers from various nations to complete Exercise 2.2 above. Trompenaars discovered that people tend to make the largest circle for the time period that their own national culture emphasized. Trompenaars also noted whether the circles overlapped, as well as the manner in which managers conceptualized the relationship between the past, present, and future (see Figure 2.1). In this example, all three time orientations were equally emphasized, and the past, present, and future exhibited linear perspective; time could not be reclaimed once an event occurred. This national study on time orientation revealed that countries such as Germany and the United States were primarily present and future oriented. Conversely, France was found to be much more focused on the past. The instructor may want to ask: Why do you think that such results occur? He might also point out that there is a heated controversy in France about overemphasizing past French achievements in school, thus diverting attention from the present and the future.

The instructor may then want to introduce Hall's concept of time. Hall distinguished between monochronic and polychronic time. Monochronic people and cultures prefer focusing on a single task at a time, and completing one task before beginning another. Polychronic cultures have the ability to focus on multiple priorities simultaneously. Table 2.3 treats additional features of monochronic and polychronic individuals and cultures.

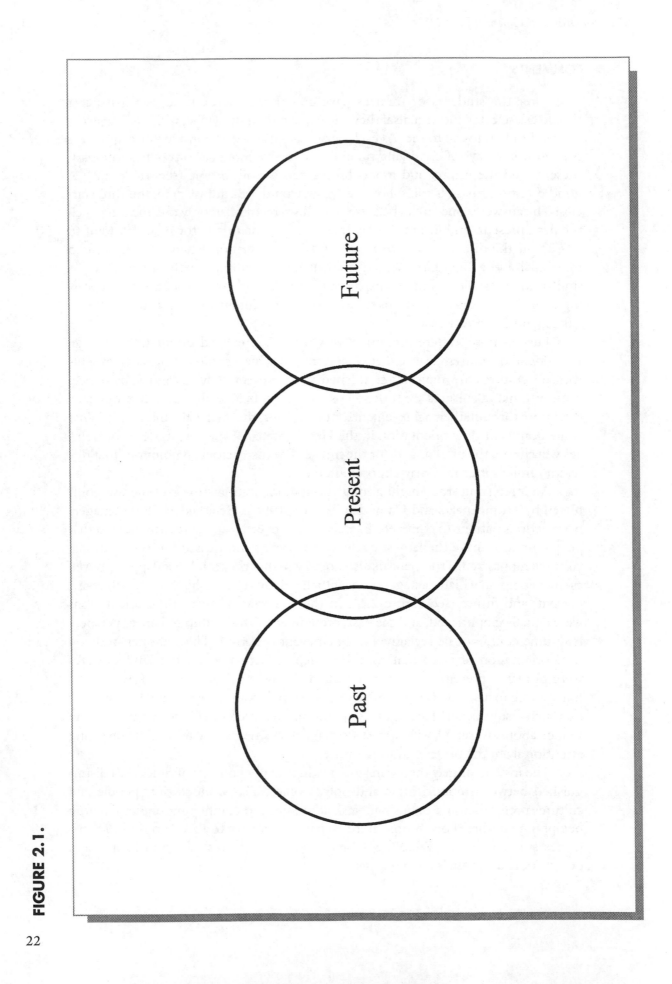

FIGURE 2.1.

TABLE 2.3: Monochronic Versus Polychronic Time

Monochronic	Polychronic
■ Does one thing at a time	■ Does many things at once
■ Makes commitments (deadlines)	■ Considers time commitments to be flexible and low priority
■ Is committed to job	■ Is committed to people and relationships
■ Concentrates on job	■ Is easily distracted
■ Emphasizes promptness	■ Bases promptness on relationships
■ Is accustomed to short-term relationships	■ Tends to form lifelong relationships
■ Is low context and needs information	■ Is high context and already has information
■ Adheres to plans	■ Changes plans often

NOTE: See Hall and Hall (1990), p. 15.

EXERCISE 2.3   **Time and National Cultures**

Ask students to select a country and then to perform an analysis of that country's time orientation. Have them indicate whether they think the country follows a linear or nonlinear (cyclical) model of time. Also have the students choose whether the country is monochronic or polychronic.

EXERCISE 2.4   **Individualism-Collectivism**

Have students think-pair-share about the concept of individualism-collectivism, and ask them to provide one specific example of both individualism and collectivism. Offer the following examples after input from each student. Briefly define individualism as the degree to which an individual will make a decision without considering or being unduly influenced by group norms (e.g., what your family considers "best" for you).

1. There is no word for "privacy" in many cultures. Or, it has a negative connotation (e.g., being cast out of a society or shunned).

2. "I" in the Japanese language is associated with words having negative meanings.

3. Several cultural groups have funeral services for those marrying outside of the group, thus signifying that they do not want to see or interact with that person.

4. Carroll and Ramamoorthy (in Carroll & Gannon, 1997) demonstrated that the individualism-collectivism orientation influences ethical behavior. For example, managers in the United States are more willing to lay off workers than are their Japanese counterparts.

EXERCISE 2.5   Collectivism and Test Taking

In a think-pair-share environment, have students discuss the following example:

> Many 18-year-old Japanese males are accompanied to their standardized college test by their mothers. The mothers wait outside until they are finished. Why does this occur? Does it happen in the United States? Would you let *your* mother do this?

The instructor can point to the critical importance of this examination for gaining admission to highly selective universities. Japanese students joke that the way to pass such tests is to give up sleep while in high school. The test tends to emphasize memorization to a much greater extent than the SAT. While in high school, many Japanese students attend a special school (*juku*) after the regular class day, after which they return home and stay up until 2 or 3 a.m. doing their regular homework. If students fail to get into an elite university, they sometimes commit suicide, in many cases because of the shame that they feel at letting down the family. Hence, test taking and collectivism are closely related.

Ironically, the Japanese students tend not to work anywhere near as much as their American counterparts during their first 2 years of college. One explanation is that these 2 years are a vacation between the regimen of secondary education and the working world. During the final 2 years of college, the students try to get into the classes of a professor-mentor, who may even help to arrange marriages. Most importantly, this professor must write a strong letter of support if the student is to obtain a desirable job after graduation.

EXERCISE 2.6   My Best Friend Versus Money

This exercise tends to generate a lively discussion. It can be related to individualism-collectivism, but more specifically to high-context collectivism. The instructor should orally provide the following incident:

> You are walking to a critical business meeting at which you are going to close a $100 million deal. You will receive a fee of three million dollars if the contract is signed. However, some

major details need to be discussed, and you are the only person capable of discussing them. Suddenly, your best friend in the world—you have known him since childhood, and he was the best man at your wedding—rushes up to you and blurts out, "Something terrible has happened, and I need your help immediately. You are the only person who can help me!" What would you do?

Typically, trainees say that they would try to identify the problem and to delay action until after the meeting. The instructor should indicate that the best friend's problem needs immediate attention. If you miss the meeting, you will probably forfeit three million dollars. Some responses are humorous and/or creative, such as splitting the fee with the friend. However, this incident brings into focus the issues of culture and values, particularly individualism-collectivism and low-context versus high-context behavior. The instructor may want to ask the class members what they would do by a show of hands. Whatever the approach, this critical incident almost always results in a spirited discussion.

EXERCISE 2.7   Space and Work

The instructor can list on the board or overhead several ways of organizing work. Rank order them in terms of the way you would prefer to work:

   a. In a separate office by yourself

   b. In an office with at least one other person

   c. In a group in which the desks are arranged so that everyone sees one another

   d. In a cubicle that allows some privacy but limited access to the other individuals in the office

■ COMMENTS

The instructor can focus the discussion by quickly tabulating the results on the blackboard or overhead. Then he or she can point out that northern Europeans tend to like to work in separate offices behind closed doors. These people and cultures view the office as an extension of their personalities. In the recent past, many offices had a light above the door. When someone knocked, the occupant of the office would press a button activating one of three lights: green (come in), yellow (wait a moment), or red (please leave).

Some extroverted people, however, do not mind sharing an office. Thus, they might select b, c, or d. Also, the Japanese tend to work in a group in which the desks are arranged so that everyone sees one another (d) and communication can occur easily across groups, as we might expect in a collectivistic culture such as Japan. The supervisor or manager sits in the front of the room and walks around it to answer questions and communicate.

Cultures also differ in terms of the placement of an office. The French manager likes to have his office in the center of the room; symbolically, power radiates from the center, and France as a nation is structured this way, with Paris as the center. American and German managers, however, prefer a corner office, possibly because of their more linear conceptions of space and time. Also, Germans tend to work behind closed office doors, whereas Americans prefer open doors if feasible. This may reflect the fact that 75% of Americans are classified as extroverted.

Today, some companies are experimenting with "borderless" offices. Everyone is in a cubicle in an open area in which they can see one another but still have sufficient privacy to hold a confidential telephone conversation. Michael Dell of Dell Computers, even though he is now ranked as one of the 10 richest Americans, works in this fashion.

EXERCISE 2.8   Spatial Zones

Edward Hall's (1968) work revealed that there are different spatial zones that cultures will use for communication. For example, among those of Anglo-Saxon heritage in the United States, there is an intimate zone that extends from 0 to 18 inches from a person. Only close relations will communicate this closely. The next zone is the comfort zone from 1½ feet to 4 feet. Communications in this zone reflect friendship and closeness. The next zone is from 4 feet to 12 feet and is reserved for impersonal communications. Outside of 12 feet is the public zone, where an individual may greet others but is unlikely to converse with anyone. However, some cultures prefer much closer contact. For example, in many Arab cultures, contact is so close that individuals frequently can smell one another's breath and odors.

Have students think-pair-share with experiences they have had where these spatial rules have been violated. Alternatively, the instructor can ask for a volunteer and can then violate the volunteer's sense of space. The discussion can focus on the volunteer's reactions and feelings.

EXERCISE 2.9   Relationship With Nature

Different cultures have distinctive views of their respective places in the world in terms of dominance of or harmony with nature, such as the conflict between the biblical belief that animals and nature are at the disposal of man, and the Indian belief that certain animals are sacred.

Other examples from various cultures include the following:

- *Ayorara*—"It can't be helped." This phrase from the Inuit in Canada indicates subjugation.

- *En Shah Allah*—If God is willing." This Muslim phrase indicates harmony with and submission to nature.

- "Just do it." This phrase expresses the American attitude of dominance over nature.

- *"Mai pen rei"*—This Thai phrase is difficult to translate but basically suggests that the individual cannot control nature.

Using the think-pair-share approach, ask the students or trainees to identify other phrases that give an indication as to the culture's attitude about their relationship with nature.

EXERCISE 2.10 Being or Doing

"Being" refers to the belief that a person should "go with the flow," accept the status quo, and enjoy the current situation. "Doing" indicates that the individual wants to change things to make them better, sets specific goals, and accomplishes them within a specific schedule.

Using think-pair-share, students should describe their ideal vacation in terms of the following:

- *Time*—a few days long or a month

- *Companions*—alone, with a few close friends, family members, or with various others

- *Living arrangements*—single rooms, shared room, or a group house

- *Activities*—rest, hiking, touring, exercising, partying

Frequently, such preferences are culturally based. For example, 75% of Americans are classified as extroverted according to the most widely used personality test, the Myers-Briggs. Hence, it is not surprising that they like to go on group vacations and, while on them, go to parties frequently. In comparison, Swedes tend to prefer to visit their *stugas,* or simple, unadorned summer homes, either alone or with just a few close friends or family members. Some Americans, hearing a Swedish friend describe such an ideal vacation, are normally very surprised, and sometimes, they compare such a vacation to going to a prison!

EXERCISE 2.11   Being and Doing Phrases

The following describe work or activities of different cultures from the perspective of being-doing:

- *Ngan*—Thai phrase for work. It is also translated as play. Thais like to punctuate their workdays with short and frequent periods of *sanuk,* or fun, during which they relax in informal groups.

- *Negocio*—Spanish phrase for work. It is translated literally in English as absence of leisure. That is, work has to be done only because it provides leisure time, during which people truly experience life to its fullest. Work is not a goal, but a means to an end.

- *Shinto blessing*—blessing of new equipment in Japanese factories. In an excellent training video, *The Kyocera Experiment* (see Chapter 9), an American engineer joins his Japanese co-workers in a Shinto ritual blessing new equipment before it is used. Later, the symbolic importance of this ritual is highlighted by a manager, who tells the workgroup, "You must learn to love your work."

- *Free time*—similar to leisure time. In Germany, this phrase would confuse a typical worker. For Germans, all time is accounted for. Work time is for work, and leisure time is for leisure.

Using think-pair-share, the instructor should ask the students to think of any phrases that may have different meanings across cultures. For example, what does "no problem" mean in Mexico and Germany? In Mexico, this phrase is used to bolster human relationships, even when there are problems and deadlines cannot be met. In Germany, "no problem" means "no problem."

EXERCISE 2.12   The Nature of People

Using think-pair-share, the instructor should ask the class to identify how different national cultures view people's inherent nature: good, bad, or a combination. In the discussion, the instructor can point out that the American view is generally positive, such as innocent until proven guilty. The French view is the opposite, or guilty until proven innocent.

EXERCISE 2.13

The Story of Upoli

Upoli was a bright and motivated Sri Lankan student who, through working very hard, was able to achieve phenomenal success in school and eventually obtain a graduate fellowship at Ohio State. He was very nervous about being a student in America and wanted to repeat his success in Sri Lanka, not only to make his parents and kinsfolk proud, but also to ensure a good position in his homeland after graduation.

At Ohio State, Upoli shared a dorm room with Jim, a rather tough but nice guy from Youngstown, Ohio. On the first day, to be polite, Upoli wakes Jim up at 6 a.m. and offers him a cup of his famous Sri Lankan tea. He repeats this offer on successive days, but Jim begins to refuse it by the fourth day. On the eighth day, Jim throws the tea into the toilet angrily, gets a cup of coffee, and tells Upoli to "go to hell."

Upoli continues to study hard, but Jim is much less interested in school. One evening, Jim comes in from a date and is a bit tipsy, and he then begins to berate Upoli for studying so hard. Jim tries to get Upoli to loosen up by getting him to agree to play billiards next Friday. But Friday comes, and Upoli says that he cannot go because he must study. This scenario occurs several times over the next few months. Jim finally blurts out in anger: "When you say you are coming, you should follow through on your word." Upoli, however, tries to explain that he must study, for to fail at school would be such a loss of face that he would never be able to return home.

Jim then invites Upoli home for Thanksgiving, and he accepts. Jim tells his parents, who make elaborate arrangements for Upoli to meet friends and relatives. At the last moment, Upoli refuses because he must study.

To complicate matters, Jim and Upoli have a difficult time communicating with one another. For instance, Jim is telling a story and Upoli will exclaim, "No!" Jim says, "What, don't you believe me? Stop saying no." At other times, Upoli exclaims, "I don't believe you!" This drives Jim crazy.

Jim's outbreaks of anger increase, and Upoli becomes so afraid that he starts to avoid him, even to the extent that he studies only in the library. Upoli makes plans to get a single room next semester. Unknown to him, so does Jim, who tells Upoli that they are too different to live together comfortably.

■ QUESTIONS

To what extent does culture explain these patterns of behavior? Do you feel that personality is as important as culture in explaining them? Why or why not? What advice would you give to Upoli so that he can avoid such problems in the future? What advice would you give to Jim? How can such communication problems be resolved?

■ COMMENTS

The instructor can use Hall's framework on low-context/high-context cultures (see Table 2.2). Losing face is literally losing an eye, a nose, and, eventually, the entire face. Saving face essentially refers to the unwritten rules that decrease this probability. Saving face is especially important in high-context cultures, for the individual has a difficult time separating his or her personality from that of the group. Thus, to lose face is to lose part of your personality and your standing in the group.

CHAPTER 3

The Dimensions of Culture: Part II

Since the end of World War II, anthropologists and, in particular, psychologists have studied the dimensions along which cultures vary, and they have found empirical support for at least 22 dimensions (Osland & Bird, 2000; see also Triandis, in press). We have already examined many of these dimensions in the previous chapter. In this chapter, the work of Geert Hofstede is highlighted first, after which work closely related to it and/or inspired by it is presented.

◧ THE WORK OF HOFSTEDE

Geert Hofstede (1980, 1991) completed a classic study of about 117,000 managers, employees, and supervisors at IBM in 53 nations. This study is cited widely and used heavily by other researchers who have related his national scores on five dimensions for each of the 53 nations to a variety of phenomena, such as the following:

- *Airline accident rates* (Phillips, 1994). Collectivistic national cultures have about three times more accidents per capita than do individualistic national cultures, and high power-distance nations have about 2½ times more accidents per capita than do low power-distance nations. The instructor may want to ask why this is so. One reasonable answer is that there is generally less openness and questioning in collectivistic and high power-distance cultures.

- *Innovation and entrepreneurship.* As a general rule, more individualistic and less uncertainty-avoidance national cultures tend to be more innovative and entrepreneurial (Franke, Hofstede, & Bond, 1991).

FIGURE 3.1: Hofstede's Dimensions of National Cultural Values in 53 Nations

Hofstede's five basic cultural dimensions across 53 nations are as follows:

- *Power distance,* or the degree to which members of a national culture automatically accept a hierarchical or unequal distribution of power in organizations and the society

- *Uncertainty avoidance,* or the degree to which members of a given national culture deal with the uncertainty and risk of everyday life and prefer to work with long-term acquaintances and friends rather than with strangers

- *Individualism-collectivism,* or the degree to which individuals in a given national culture perceive themselves as separate from others and free from group pressure to conform

- *Masculinity,* or the degree to which a national culture looks favorably on aggressive and materialistic behavior

- *Time orientation,* or the degree to which members of a national culture will defer gratification to achieve long-term success (short-term to long-term)

FIGURE 3.2: Hofstede's Rank Ordering of 53 Nations on Five Cultural Dimensions, Going From 1 (Highest) to 53 (Lowest)

Nation	Power Distance	Individualism	Masculinity	Uncertainty Avoidance	Time Horizon (1 = long)[a]
Germany	42-44	15	9-10	29	11-12
Sweden	47-48	10-11	52	49-50	10
England	42-44	3	9-10	47-48	15-16
Australia	41	2	16	37	11-12
U.S.	38	1	15	43	14
Italy	34	7	4-5	23	—
India	10-11	21	20-21	45	6
Japan	33	22-23	1	7	3
Taiwan	29-30	44	32-33	26	2
Hong Kong	15-16	37	18-19	49-50	1
South Korea	27-28	43	41	16-17	4
Arab nations	7	26-27	23	27	—

a. For this dimension, information is available on only 22 of the 53 nations (Hofstede & Bond, 1988).

Other advantages of Hofstede's five dimensions (see Figure 3.1) include the fact that they are based on prominent psychological and sociological theories within the American and European traditions that are well over 100 years old; they are empirically derived; they allow us to rank order nations on each dimension; and they are readily understandable by managers and students. Hofstede's prominence is reflected by the fact that he recently surpassed Karl Marx as the most cited researcher in the Social Science Citation Index. Also, subsequent research has continued to refine his dimensions (Smith & Bond, 1998).

EXERCISE 3.1

Continuing to Use Hofstede's Dimensions

After explaining Hofstede's five dimensions in Figure 3.1, the instructor can list two to seven nations from Figure 3.2 on the blackboard or on a blank overhead. Ask the students or trainees to indicate where each nation ranks in terms of Hofstede's five dimensions, and then show Figure 3.2. As a general rule, students and trainees interested in global affairs tend to rank each nation on the same dimensions in a manner similar to what Hofstede's research indicates.

EXERCISE 3.2   **Supplementing Hofstede's Framework**

Students and managerial trainees typically absorb Hofstede's study without questioning it. The instructor can ask students: What is incomplete about Hofstede's approach, or, more correctly, why is it important but incomplete by itself?

■ COMMENTS

Typically, the discussion is limited at this point, but the instructor can point out the following deficiencies:

- The scores and rank orderings of some countries, such as England and the United States, are very similar, although practical experience suggests that there are vast differences between them (see Figure 3.2).

- There are many different types of individualism and of collectivism, such as the competitive individualism found in the United States and the egalitarian form associated with Australia (see Figure 3.3).

- Although Hofstede's dimensions, which are based on only 22 questionnaire items, provide an effective overall approach for comparing the cultures of nations, they are not grounded to specific nations, that is, they do not provide a rich understanding of a nation's culture in the manner that is frequently associated with cultural anthropology. His dimensions are designed to be etic, or culture-general, rather than emic, or culture-specific.

▀ IDIOCENTRISM AND ALLOCENTRISM

There has been some important work on cross-cultural dimensions since Hofstede's original analysis. In particular, Shalom Schwartz's work has been widely recognized as being an important advance over Hofstede's work, and Hofstede has praised this work publicly (see Smith & Schwartz, 1996). Schwartz pointed out that Hofstede could not analyze the Communist nations. Hence, Schwartz included a number of former Communist nations in his survey. He also asked cross-cultural psychologists in 55 nations to contribute items to his survey. Schwartz asked students and teachers to complete his survey of values because he believes that they are most expressive of a nation's values.

Furthermore, Schwartz completed two levels of analyses. For the national cultural level, he added together the scores of individuals. However, he agreed with Hofstede that individuals within a specific culture can deviate from the national cultural norms. For example, although the national culture may be highly individualistic, particular individuals within it may be highly collectivistic or allocentric. Similarly, the culture may be collectivistic, but particular individuals in it may be highly individualistic or idiocentric. In general, Schwartz's cultural-level analysis supported Hofstede's dimensions. But Schwartz's individual level of analysis provides data not available in Hofstede's work.

FIGURE 3.3: Specific Types of Individualism and Collectivism

Individualism

German symphony: Subordinated individualism, that is, subordinating individual goals to group goals

Italian opera: Exteriorized individualism, that is, expressing individual thoughts and emotions but within the context of the family and community

Traditional British house: Tradition-bound and iconoclastic individualism

Spanish bullfight: Proud and self-sufficient individualism, where the focus is working only as a gang, not as a group with collective goals

American football: Competitive individualism

Swedish stuga: Individualism through nature and self-development

French wine: Rationalistic individualism

Irish conversations: Religion-focused individualism

Collectivism

Chinese family altar: Relation-based and differentiated family system

Japanese garden: Kata-based undifferentiated family system

Indian Dance of Shiva: Religion-dominated family system

Israeli kibbutz and moshav: Democracy-based family system

SOURCE: Gannon and Associates (1994).

EXERCISE 3.3   **Idiocentrism and Allocentrism**

After presenting this link between the cultural and individual levels of analysis, the instructor should place Figure 3.4 on the blackboard or overhead. Ask the students to analyze the four cells in terms of the degree to which cooperativeness is maximized, using the think-pair-share method.

■ **COMMENTS**

As part of the class discussion, the instructor should go over a study completed by Chatman and Barsade (1995). They randomly assigned allocentrics and idiocentrics to simulated collectivistic and individualistic cultures. Cooperation was

FIGURE 3.4. Individualism and Collectivism at Two Levels

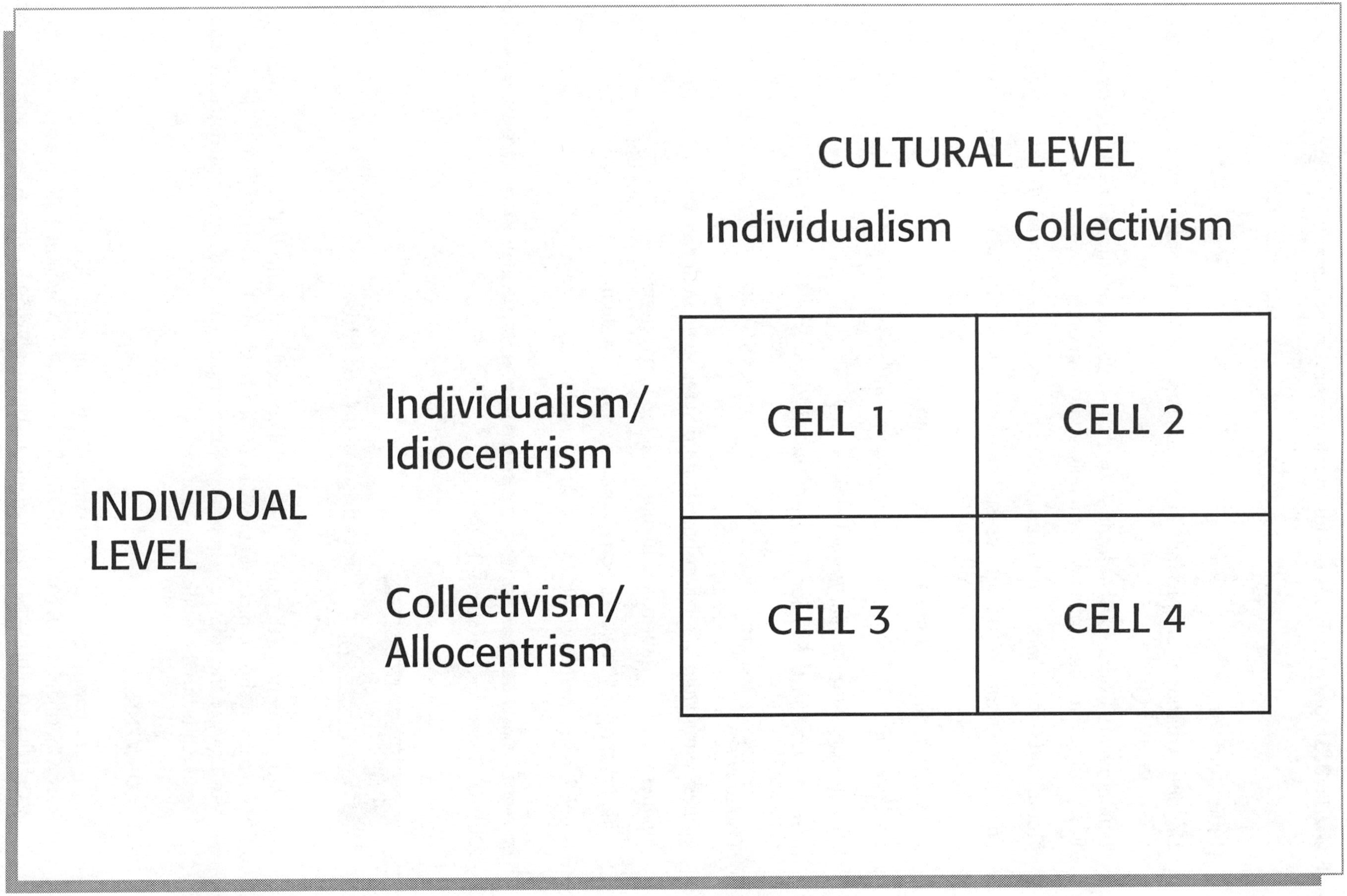

CULTURAL LEVEL

	Individualism	Collectivism
Individualism/ Idiocentrism	CELL 1	CELL 2
Collectivism/ Allocentrism	CELL 3	CELL 4

INDIVIDUAL LEVEL

highest in Cell 4, that is, allocentrics in a collectivist culture. However, allocentrics were low on cooperation when assigned to an individualistic culture (Cell 3). Idiocentrics assigned to the collectivistic culture were cooperative (Cell 2), but when assigned to individualistic cultures, they were low on cooperation (Cell 1).

The instructor may want to follow up by asking the students why these results occurred.

◼ SHARED CULTURAL VALUES

The most fundamental concept in cross-cultural studies is that of shared values. Hofstede's five dimensions reflect such national cultural values. A more specific analysis of values is provided by George England (1975). He analyzed management values and how they varied by national culture. Through his work, he was able to characterize managers as pragmatic, moralistic, affective (feeling), or a combination of the three. England studied five nations in depth: the United States, Japan, Korea, Australia, and India. He provides the following definitions for these characterizations:

- The *pragmatic* mode suggests that an individual has an evaluative framework that is guided primarily by considerations of success or failure. Will a certain course of action work or not? How successful or unsuccessful is it likely to be?

- The *ethical-moral* mode implies an evaluative framework consisting of ethical considerations that influence behavior toward actions and decisions that are judged to be "right" and away from those judged to be "wrong."

- The *affect* or *feeling* evaluation suggests an evaluative framework that is guided by hedonism; one behaves in ways that can increase pleasure and decrease pain.

England's findings indicate that the highest and second highest percentage of managers falling into each of the three categories for these five nations is as follows (note that percentages for managers from each nation would add up to 100 if all data were presented):

- 67.4% pragmatic among the Japanese, and 15.8% a combination of the three modes

- 57.3% pragmatic among the Americans, but 30.3% moralistic

- 53.1% pragmatic among the Koreans, and 29.4% a combination of the three modes

- 40.2% pragmatic among the Australians, but 40.2% moralistic

- 44.1% moralistic among the Indians, but 34.0% pragmatic

As these data indicate, fewer than 10% of the managers from any of these nations fell into the affect mode. Given the importance of the pragmatic and moralistic modes, the instructor may want to ask class members to identify tensions that may arise between managers emphasizing one of them to the exclusion of the others.

<table>
<tr><td>EXERCISE 3.4</td><td>Cultural Values</td></tr>
</table>

Employing think-pair-share, the instructor should ask the students to profile each of these five nations in terms of one or more of these three orientations. The nations are listed on page 37.

CHAPTER 4

Cultural Metaphors

The work of Kluckholn and Strodtbeck, Hall, Hofstede, and many others who study national cross-cultural differences has been invaluable in the area of cross-cultural studies. Their dimensions of culture constitute a base upon which a majority of more recent studies have been built. However, as discussed in Chapter 3, their work in some regards is incomplete.

For example, Hofstede was able to rank nations according to their scores on several dimensions. Using this method, he was able to draw a conclusion that England and the United States were very similar. However, anyone even remotely familiar with England and the United States knows that vast differences exist, and to apply Hofstede's perspective without taking into account those differences would be risky. It seems feasible to supplement the dimensional studies with another approach. Along these lines, Gannon and his colleagues have argued that the dimensional approach should be supplemented by a more content-rich or grounded approach, that of cultural metaphors (see Gannon & Audia, in press).

■ USING METAPHORS TO UNDERSTAND NATIONAL DIFFERENCES

A cultural metaphor is some unique or distinctive institution, phenomenon, or activity expressive of a nation's values, such as the Chinese family altar or American football. Frequently, outsiders have difficulty understanding such metaphors and the manner in which they express values. Also, members of a culture tend to be emotionally expressive about their cultural metaphors.

A study completed by Gannon and Associates (1997) used surveys to analyze in-depth the accuracy of six of the cultural metaphors for England, Germany, India, Italy, Taiwan, and the United States. (See Figures 4.1, 4.2, and 4.3.) In order to validate each metaphor, researchers posed two overarching research questions. First, did the respondents from a particular country identify with the items whose underlying factors were similar to those of the metaphors from which they were generated? Second, could subjects distinguish between items describing their culture and those describing another culture?

In these three separate surveys, at the top of the page was the phrase *"Most people in my country:"* followed by items designed as sentence fragments to complete the sentence and record the subject's response. These items were based on the work of Gannon and Associates (1994). Subjects were college students, and there was a total of 664: Seventy-two were from the United States, 130 from India, 64 from England, 192 from Taiwan, 65 from Germany, and 141 from Italy. Two nations were compared in each instance: The United States and India, England and Taiwan, and Germany and Italy. Thus, there were three different questionnaires.

The results of this study were generally supportive of the metaphorical approach to describing culture. However, metaphors should be used with caution. Metaphors do not pertain to every individual or even every subgroup within a society. Rather, they highlight national differences in an easily understood way that provides a rich vocabulary for any discussions. This is in contrast to the quantitative dimensional studies, such as Hofstede's, whose results are often hard to remember and difficult to use in daily cultural interactions. In addition, a cultural metaphor provides nation-specific characteristics rather than general dimensions along which all nations vary.

EXERCISE 4.1   Questionnaire Items

The instructor should review the information presented above with the class. Then, the instructor should break the class into six groups. If the class is large, it can be divided into any number of groups that is a multiple of six. Groups should work outside of class if possible.

Each group should be assigned one of the following six nations: the United States, India, England, Taiwan, Germany, or Italy. The group should develop questionnaire items for its assigned nation. Each group should prepare an overhead on which its items are listed. The instructor can then show on an overhead the items developed by the research team.

The instructor should show Figure 4.1 on an overhead. He or she can then ask class members about each questionnaire item, that is, the degree to which it represents the United States on a 0-10 scale, and then the degree to which it represents India. The same procedure can be employed for Figures 4.2 and 4.3.

In the event that students have not read the chapters pertaining to all six countries, the group assigned to work on one nation can serve as the expert in this exercise.

■ COMMENTS

Through these activities, students can gain an appreciation of the manner in which culture can be studied; cultural metaphors can be created; and the methods by which such concepts can be confirmed, disconfirmed, or refined.

FIGURE 4.1. Questionnaire Items: United States and India

Cultural Metaphor for the United States: American Football

Cultural Metaphor for India: The Dance of Shiva

Please indicate, by filling in *any single number between 0 and 10,* the degree to which you feel each statement or description represents the United States. Then, alongside this rating, please indicate the degree to which you feel each item represents India. Use 0 for *do not agree at all* and 10 for *totally agree,* or any number in between.

Most people in my country would agree that:

_____ All existence is cyclical, that is, it originates, exists, becomes chaotic, and is destroyed, and then begins again.

_____ The world as we know it is illusory.

_____ The aim of life is to realize the illusory nature of existence and achieve salvation from the cycle of birth and death.

_____ Many paths can lead to the same end of salvation.

_____ Innovation and modification of existing practices are encouraged.

_____ People are generally open to change.

_____ There is quick acceptance and use of new technology.

_____ There is belief in individual liberty.

_____ There is belief in equality of opportunity for all.

_____ Values and ideals include independence, initiative, and self-reliance.

_____ People tend to be extroverted, energetic, and motivated.

_____ Personal success or failure is attributed to the efforts of the individual.

_____ Attention is given to the nuclear, rather than the extended, family.

_____ Competition is protected and enhanced.

_____ Political authority is subject to checks and balances.

_____ People are ready to defy authority if they feel wronged.

_____ Efforts are focused primarily on short-term issues.

_____ Life consists of four stages—student, householder, retiree, and a person who has renounced the world.

_____ All acts or deeds have consequences, and it is the sum total of positive and negative deeds that will determine progress through the passage of life.

FIGURE 4.1. Continued

____ Deeds should be performed in accordance with the religiously prescribed ways.

____ Life is uncertain and risky.

____ Uncertainty in life can be reduced through astrology.

____ Differences are put aside temporarily and cooperation is encouraged when people are faced with difficult problems and goals.

____ Group relationships are cooperative but only superficially friendly.

____ You are judged by what you are doing and the goals you are accomplishing.

____ Jobs, careers, and geographic region are changed throughout life.

____ One's place in society is earned rather than prescribed.

____ Anyone with motivation and ability can get ahead regardless of his or her personal background.

____ There is belief that any problem can be solved.

____ Kinship systems primarily define in-groups and out-groups.

____ Geographical origin secondarily defines in-groups and out-groups.

____ Personal identity is based significantly on the reputation of the family and kinship group.

____ The individual is capable of anything he or she wants to accomplish.

____ Time is limited, so things should be done quickly.

____ Winning, fame, and glory are important.

____ This country is superior to most, if not all, other nations.

____ The nation's freedom should be preserved and protected above all other considerations.

____ We celebrate our national feeling voluntarily by displaying flags in many places and by joining in singing the national anthem on many occasions.

____ Family and kinship networks define one's life and perspective.

____ Ability counts much less than family and kinship connections in the world of work.

____ Lifestyles and actions are more the result of family circumstances and kinship groupings than individual choice.

____ Age and gender are major influences on the patterns and depth of interactions among individuals.

FIGURE 4.1. Continued

_____ Permanent inequality of different social groups is inevitable.

_____ Working hard, while it may be valued, is less important than maintaining relationships and meeting familial and kinship obligations.

_____ Working hard, while it may be valued, is less important than social class membership in getting ahead at work.

_____ Favoritism toward family members is viewed as fulfilling one's duties to the family and kinship group.

_____ Institutional change in the workplace is difficult because of the enormous power that is frequently accorded to leaders.

FIGURE 4.2. Cross-Cultural Questionnaire Items: England and Taiwan

Cultural Metaphor for England: The Traditional British Home

Cultural Metaphor for Taiwan: The Chinese Family Altar

Please indicate, by filling in *any single number between 0 and 10,* the degree to which you feel each statement or description represents England. Then, alongside this rating, please indicate the degree to which you feel each item represents Taiwan. Use 0 for *do not agree at all* and 10 for *totally agree,* or any number in between.

Most people in my country:

_____ are patient.

_____ are publicly unexcitable.

_____ are orderly.

_____ are modest.

_____ deemphasize theory in favor of collecting data and observations.

_____ are very polite and phrase issues and questions so as not to offend.

_____ feel strongly that the nation should be free of foreign domination.

_____ are individualistic within the constraints of tradition and society's norms.

_____ value a wry sense of humor.

_____ would agree that the family is more important than anything else.

_____ would agree that the family tends to be patriarchal and conservative.

_____ would agree that praying to ancestors is helpful.

_____ would agree that it is important to have sons to carry on the family name and carry out family responsibilities.

_____ would agree that having primarily or only family members in a family business, especially in positions of authority, is the preferred way of organizing a business.

_____ would agree that it is best to take a long-term approach, perhaps as long as 100 years, to issues and problems.

_____ would agree that time is circular; that is, the past, present, and future are bound within one another.

_____ are taught from an early age to control spontaneity and to follow detailed manners.

_____ are taught from an early age to know their place in society.

_____ readily identify with one social class.

FIGURE 4.2. Continued

_____ differentiate social classes through details of speech, manner, dress, and occupation.

_____ prefer to stick with tried and tested ways of doing things.

_____ would agree that achieving harmony in the family and kinship group is of overriding consideration.

_____ would agree that everyone's dignity should be safeguarded whenever possible.

_____ would agree that the winner in a contest or negotiation should allow the loser to save as much face as possible.

_____ place a high value on playing fairly.

_____ identify with the underdog rather than the favorite.

_____ respect law and order to such a degree that they expect that almost everyone else in the country will automatically know and follow the rules of society, even if those rules are not written.

_____ would agree that a person should normally act independently only after the specific responsibilities involving family and kinship group members are carried out.

_____ would agree that it is good to be innovative and entrepreneurial as long as the family and kinship group obligations are carried out.

_____ would agree that achieving material progress in life is important because it ensures the respect of your children and ancestors.

_____ would agree that material success is a way of honoring your ancestors.

FIGURE 4.3. Cross-Cultural Questionnaire Items: Germany and Italy

Cultural Metaphor for Germany: The Symphony

Cultural Metaphor for Italy: The Opera

Please indicate, by filling in *any single number between 0 and 10,* the degree to which you feel each statement or description represents Germany. Then, alongside this rating, please indicate the degree to which you feel each item represents Italy. Use 0 for *do not agree at all* and 10 for *totally agree,* or any number in between.

Most people in my country:

____ forcefully assert their position within the constraint of agreed-upon rules.

____ do not like to stand out too much from others in a group.

____ view it as a responsibility to voluntarily subdue individual preference for the greater good of the whole.

____ value rules and order.

____ will correct people, even in public, if rules are ignored.

____ believe that everyone has a set place in the structure of society.

____ would agree that everyone has a responsibility to fulfill his or her role in society.

____ are very concerned with the impression they make on others, such as through flattery, making promises, and embellishing events.

____ try to impress others by flaunting material possessions and dressing well without giving offense.

____ pay great attention to surface appearances; they do not dig too deeply into things.

____ prefer leaders who approach problems without emotions.

____ prefer to work in departments that are relatively autonomous in decision-making authority.

____ prefer a high degree of functional specialization.

____ when making an argument, like to collect and present extensive amounts of background information.

____ agree that leaders, when heading departments, possess unquestioned authority on most issues.

____ reach decisions through consensus when dealing with other departments.

____ love colorful rituals and spectacles.

____ love and react strongly to emotional dramas and celebrations.

FIGURE 4.3. Continued

_____ are great spectators of life in public places.

_____ value punctuality and are conscious of time.

_____ make a sharp distinction between work and leisure and do not socialize with co-workers after work as a sharp distinction between friends and acquaintances is made.

_____ are generally formal when introducing and meeting others and reserve informality for close friends and family.

_____ value their privacy, which cannot be breached without an invitation.

_____ are highly expressive with others—they chat, whistle, swear, sing, weep, and laugh.

_____ consider the way they speak (tone, passion, rhythm, volume) to be as important as what is actually said.

_____ talk with their hands, arms, shoulders, and facial expression as much as with words.

_____ tend to reveal their thoughts and emotions to others rather than keeping them private.

_____ base their personal identity more on family affiliation than on affiliation with employers or political parties.

_____ regard the family dinner as the center of life.

_____ trust family members more than anyone else to give them true information and to protect them against troubles.

EXERCISE 4.2   Paragraph Profiles

For each of the six nations highlighted in Exercise 4.1-4.3, the researchers also developed two one-paragraph profiles, two per nation. In one paragraph, the cultural metaphor is not mentioned; in the other, it is mentioned explicitly (see Figures 4.4, 4.5, and 4.6). The instructor can ask each small group to prepare two such paragraphs for one of six nations outside of class, one with the cultural metaphor explicitly mentioned and one without it. These paragraphs can then be compared to those created by the researchers.

As a related exercise, the students can use a 0-10 scale to indicate the degree to which they feel each paragraph in Figure 4.4 represents the United States. Then, using the same scale, they can indicate the degree to which each paragraph represents India. The same procedures apply to England and Taiwan, and Germany and Italy (Figures 4.5 and 4.6).

Alternatively, the instructor can place Figure 4.4 on an overhead. Using the think-pair-share method, the instructor can ask class members to identify the nation being described in each paragraph, and why class members have identified specific nations with specific paragraphs. The instructor should specify the identity of the two nations in this exercise (United States and India). He or she can repeat this activity for Figure 4.4 and 4.6.

◤ USING CULTURAL METAPHORS TO IMPLEMENT ORGANIZATIONAL CHANGE

Pearce and Osmond (1996), in their article titled "Metaphors for Change: The ALP (Access Leverage Points) Model of Change Management," endorse the use of cultural metaphors to assist in implementing organizational change across nations. Specifically, they recommend that managers can implement complex organizational change more effectively by pinpointing ALPs from that nation's culture. They suggest that these ALPs are critical aspects of the nation's culture that can often aid, but sometimes impede, the introduction and management of organizational change. This article is reprinted in Gannon (2001).

Use of Pearce and Osmond's model is intended to give change agents more cultural awareness for the organization with which they are working. Also, the model should allow change agents to develop specific strategies for the facilitation of change.

Their process has three steps: (a) identification of a metaphor to describe the culture of a particular nation, (b) identification of ALPs within the metaphor framework, and (c) development of intervention strategies (2 to 5) to deal with each ALP. Figure 4.7 shows an example of their work, taken from the Gannon and Associates (1994) metaphor for England (The Traditional British House).

FIGURE 4.4. Paragraph Profiles: United States and India

Please indicate, by filling in *any single number between 0 and 10,* the degree to which you feel each statement or description represents the United States. Then, alongside this rating, please indicate the degree to which you feel each item represents India. Use 0 for *do not agree at all* and 10 for *totally agree,* or any number in between.

_____ Most people in my culture would agree that this nation's culture revolves around religion and family/kinship groupings. The major themes in the culture are predetermination of life (destiny) and the cyclicality of life activities, stressing origination, existence, chaos, destruction, and then reorganization. All deeds and acts are seen as having consequences that can extend beyond earthly existence. Duties associated with kinship groupings are defined clearly. There is a strong in-group orientation based on kinship groups that emphasizes the hierarchical relationships within the group based on age and gender. Between kinship groups, there is a clearly demarcated hierarchy that subsumes other bases for differentiating people, such as race, language, and geographical origin.

_____ Most people in my country would agree that there is intense competition, constant geographic movement, and continual striving to improve one's position in life in this culture. There is a high degree of individual specialization, a pervading sense of urgency, and rapid acceptance of new technology in this society. The individual is the most important unit within society; people have a strong concern for protecting their rights as individuals and are ready to defy authority if they feel wronged by decisions that may affect them. There is a belief that the individual is capable of anything he or she wants to accomplish if he or she sets his or her mind to it. As a result, people are mobile, energetic, and motivated to achieve specific goals. People generally pursue their own personal interests but will cooperate with each other to achieve specific goals. Personal success or failure is generally attributed to the efforts of the individual, and there is celebration of winners.

_____ Most people in my country would view life as a celestial dance. The dance represents the cyclical nature of the philosophy based in origination, existence that slowly slides into chaos, and, finally, destruction, so that the cycle can start all over again. Notions of transmigration of the soul, concepts of acts or deeds, and concepts of duty are represented by the dance. The emphasis of the people is on doing their duty, which is limited and oriented toward the family and kinship network.

_____ The value of my culture could be compared to a competitive game in which there is intense competition, speed, constant movement, and a sense of limited time. Individuals have highly specialized roles, and team members cooperate to achieve specific, short-term goals. Anyone can play on the team based on his or her ability and performance rather than on personal background. There is a clear delineation between winners and losers; winning is often accompanied by great celebration.

FIGURE 4.5. Paragraph Profiles: England and Taiwan

Please indicate, by filling in *any single number between 0 and 10,* the degree to which you feel each statement or description represents England. Then, alongside this rating, please indicate the degree to which you feel each item represents Taiwan. Use 0 for *do not agree at all* and 10 for *totally agree,* or any number in between.

____ Most people in my country would agree that a stone or brick house is an appropriate metaphor for this nation's culture because of its projection of stability, fortitude, sense of order and permanence, traditions, a glorious history, and stable social identification.

____ Most people in my country would agree that the nation's culture is based on strong, patriarchal, and conservative families and kinship groups that greatly value hard work and planning for future generations. In this culture, living family members show great respect for elder and deceased family members, and they pray to their deceased family members to help them with their problems, thus emphasizing the continuity and structural completeness of the family over many generations. Relationships between family members—for example, husband and wife, and older brother and younger brother—and the responsibilities flowing directly from these relationships are critical, and the goal is to achieve harmony for all while safeguarding their dignity. Because relationships are so close and specific, if there is a family business, it is difficult for family members to integrate nonfamily individuals into it.

____ Most people in my country would agree that the nation's culture emphasizes the development of a strong, patient, and publicly unexcitable personality. There is a preference for individuals who mostly adhere to tradition, but harmless eccentric individuals are accepted. Emotional outbursts are generally frowned upon, psychological distance between individuals is prized, and patience is held in high honor. Playing fair is stressed, encouraging the underdog rather than favorites is viewed positively, and shunning abstract theory in favor of previously used practical solutions is favored. This nation's culture also emphasizes modesty, wry humor, communication that is circumspect, politeness, and phrasing questions and issues so as to avoid confrontation.

____ Most people in my country would agree that a family shrine or altar clearly reflects the basic values of the country's culture because of its emphasis on respecting and praying to ancestors, seeking harmonious relationships in the family and kinship group while safeguarding everyone's dignity, and building for the future while maintaining solid traditions.

FIGURE 4.6. Paragraph Profiles: Germany and Italy

Please indicate, by filling in *any single number between 0 and 10*, the degree to which you feel each statement or description represents Germany. Then, alongside this rating, please indicate the degree to which you feel each item represents Italy. Use 0 for *do not agree at all* and 10 for *totally agree*, or any number in between.

_____ Most people in my country would agree that in this culture, there is an emphasis on rules and order. The manager or administrator of a group unites the disparate personalities, perspectives, and talents in order to achieve a unified and combined effort toward a common goal. Individuals in a group do not necessarily want to be the center of attention. Rather, the individual sees it as his or her responsibility to contribute to the success of the whole. There exists a responsibility to abide by legitimate authority. In this culture, there is a clear separation between private and public life, which goes along with the clear distinction between friendship and colleagueship.

_____ Most people in my country are greatly concerned with the impression they make on others through flattery, material possessions, and dramatic impact. They love to watch colorful, emotional spectacles and rituals. They tend to be very emotionally open and expressive with others and make extensive use of body language to communicate. Also, they tend to derive their identity, trust, and sense of security mainly from the immediate family.

_____ Most people in my country would agree that one can compare this nation with a symphony orchestra because of its emphasis on order, rules, regularity, punctuality, and submission of the individual to group goals. In addition, the symphony orchestra combines various types of musicians, styles, and perspectives; it produces a unified sound. The conductor brings the diverse instruments into concert or combined effort just as the manager or administrator does.

_____ Most people in this country tend to view opera as a suitable cultural metaphor because of its emphasis on spectacle, pageantry, the lyrical use of language, and the inevitable expression of thoughts and emotions to others within the family and outside of it.

FIGURE 4.7. Summary of the British Cultural Metaphor (The Traditional British House), Access Leverage Points (ALPs), and Intervention Strategies

Step 1 *The Submetaphorical* *Constructs*	*Step 2* *The Access* *Leverage Points*	*Step 3* *The Intervention* *Strategies*
Historical Foundations of Great Britain	Acceptance of Tradition	Identify relevant traditions Demonstrate how the change builds upon traditions Involve people in the change to embrace ownership
	Subtlety of Language	Discount overt stimuli Pay strict attention to subtle clues Engage in diplomatic behavior
Socialization in Great Britain	Probity of Position	Ensure contact at appropriate level Demonstrate top man- agement commitment Involve key stakeholders
	Use of Ceremony	Involve top management in ceremonies Use ceremonies to mark the beginning of change Employ symbolism and ritual
Awareness of Traditions as a Way of Life in Great Britain	Disposition Toward Rules	Specify rules precisely Specify rules as guidelines Build upon existing rules

SOURCE: Pearce and Osmond (1996).

EXERCISE 4.3   Organizational Change

Using the Pearce-Osmond method, have groups of students develop a similar table for a nation of their choice.

EXERCISE 4.4   Learning About Cultural Metaphors in Pairs or Triads

The instructor may want to require that each student read only part of the book *Understanding Global Cultures.* Students or trainees can learn about all of the cultural metaphors described in this book through the creation of pairs, triads, and other small group combinations.

Each student in a pair should read half of the book. He or she is responsible for explaining each of his or her assigned chapters orally to the other group member. The student should be sure to outline the metaphor, the dimensions, and where the nation ranks in the measurement of various cultural dimensions. One student in each small group should explain his or her chapter, and time should be allotted for discussion. Then the second student does the same. They continue in this fashion, either in the classroom or outside of it, until all of the assigned chapters have been covered.

EXERCISE 4.5   Cultural Sensemaking

Dr. Joyce Osland and Dr. Maggie Phillips developed this exercise for the 1998 Biannual International Meeting of the Western Academy of Management in Istanbul, Turkey. Although it was used to understand Turkish culture, cultural sensemaking can be applied to any culture.

At the first meeting, the instructor provides background reading, for example, the Turkish coffeehouse (Gannon & Associates, 2001). Teams of four or five people are formed. Preferably at least two of these people do not know the others, and at least one should be non-American. Team members should introduce themselves. Each team member should then identify something in the target culture about which he or she would like to learn on a firsthand basis (e.g., attitudes toward work and nonwork activities, specific cross-cultural dimensions such as power distance and uncertainty avoidance, etc.).

After the team has agreed on the topics to be studied, its members develop interview items that they will use in interviewing two or three natives. Then, team members complete the interviews. This approach guarantees a small but rich database.

The team meets once again and pools its information. It then creates an overhead or a large white sheet of paper that can be posted on the wall summarizing the collected information. Teams then report their conclusions to the class.

In this sensemaking exercise, the cultural metaphor is used as the starting point. As information is collected, the team members should develop a richer and more refined understanding of the culture. This manner of using cultural metaphors is recommended by Gannon and Associates (2001).

EXERCISE 4.6   **Stereotypes and Cultural Metaphors**

The goal of this exercise is to show how a stereotype differs from a cultural metaphor. Using think-pair-share, the instructor should ask the students to answer the following questions:

- What is a stereotype?

- Is a stereotype necessarily bad?

- How do cultural metaphors differ from stereotypes?

■ COMMENTS

In their extreme form, stereotypes are a universal syllogism, placing individuals into categories for which no exceptions are allowed, except at the margins. For example, note the following:

- All Xs are stupid.

- John is an X.

- Thus, John is stupid.

Are stereotypes necessarily bad? According to Adler (1991), not if they are

- a first best guess;

- based on data and observation;

- descriptive rather than evaluative;

- open to change if new data are encountered.

By definition, a stereotype phrased as a universal syllogism is inaccurate.

A cultural metaphor differs from a stereotype because it refers to a group (ethnic, national, etc.) but is only probabilistic. Thus, a cultural metaphor allows for exceptions and does not include every individual or even every subgroup. However, stereotypes and cultural metaphors do overlap. See Gannon and Associates (2001), Chapter 1, for further discussion.

EXERCISE 4.7   The Cultural Interview

Each member of the class should select one chapter from Gannon and Associates (2001), such as the Chinese Family Altar. He or she should develop a series of interview items based on the selected culture and then interview an individual from that culture. He or she can summarize the results in a short paper and/or a class presentation.

An alternative format is to assign one cultural metaphor to a small group of four or five students. Then, the group can construct a common interview guide that everyone will use, and summarize the results in a paper and/or a class presentation.

EXERCISE 4.8   Debating the Merits of Cultural Metaphors

Students or trainees should be assigned to small groups. One set of groups should describe the strengths and weaknesses of cultural metaphors. A second set of groups should describe the strengths and weaknesses of cross-cultural dimensions, particularly Hofstede's well-known five dimensions (see Figure 3.1). Each small group should prepare an overhead. Finally, the instructor can show Figure 4.8. Professor Michele Gelfand used this comparative approach in a lively class debate that took place in her cross-cultural course at the University of Maryland, and Figure 4.8 was the result.

Alternatively, the instructor can use the think-pair-share method, asking first about the strengths and weaknesses of cultural metaphors and then about cross-cultural dimensions.

EXERCISE 4.9   Creating Advertising Slogans

This exercise helps students and trainees gain a quick understanding of the usefulness of cultural metaphors. They also begin to realize that cross-cultural behavior is of more than theoretical interest. First, the instructor reviews the material in Figure 4.9, which summarizes the cultural metaphors and their specific dimensions for five

FIGURE 4.8. Summary of Class Debate

METAPHORS

General Strengths:

- Afford a rich, detailed, in-depth understanding of a culture. May include elements not captured in dimensional approach.

- Afford a dynamic view of culture, which includes actual experience and vivid images that capture many of the senses. Can help see how people participate in culture.

- Provide an integrated view of culture that captures the interrelationships among dimensions and how they relate to behavior.

- Are very useful for cross-cultural training. Allow for an understanding of the host's perspective and may enhance perspective taking and empathy.

- Are very useful for research in early stages (gaining understanding, for both theory and method).

General Weaknesses:

- Do not easily allow for comparisons.

- Are not empirically verified (as of yet).

- Describing cultures in terms of one metaphor is simplistic and will miss important elements of the cultures. By definition, metaphors highlight some aspects of reality and ignore others.

- Are more susceptible to stereotyping, and it may be harder to change stereotypes (compared to dimensions) because they are vivid and may stick.

- Some metaphorical mappings may be a "stretch."

- Metaphors have been discussed mainly at the cultural level.

- **They need the dimensional approach.**

FIGURE 4.8. Continued

DIMENSIONS

General Strengths:

- Allow for a "common metric" to compare cultures and a structure to understand an immense amount of detail.

- Are quantifiable. Can derive specific dimensions and measures, and can be used to predict psychological phenomena.

- Are verifiable. Procedures are available to validate whether ranking of cultures supports theory.

- Are amenable to large-scale, multicountry studies, where cultures can be compared (assuming methodological pitfalls have been accounted for).

- Enable us to see similarities across different cultures that may not have been expected (i.e., Japan and United States on M/F).

- May allow for more distance to view culture and elicit less negative reactions.

- Have been researched at the individual and cultural levels.

General Weaknesses:

- It is hard to keep the Hofstede 5-dimensional model of culture in mind.

- We often look at one dimension separately, yet culture is a complex whole, and psychological phenomena are multiply determined.

- Dimensions can be atheoretical (i.e., always need theory regarding why dimensions exist).

- Research in cross-cultural psychology tends to examine one dimension (I/C).

- Dimensions are extremely broad and miss important elements.

- They can obfuscate within-culture diversity and dynamics of culture.

- **They need the metaphor approach.**

NOTE: M/F = Masculinity/Femininity, or Degree of Aggressiveness; I/C = Individualism/Collectivism.

nations. The instructor may also want to use Figure 3.3, which delineates specific types of individualism and collectivism. Students will then write an advertising slogan for use in one of the cultures.

To introduce the exercise, the instructor points out that more than 10% of all jobs in the United States are in tourism and travel-related industries, and that this is the largest industry in the world. Then, the instructor breaks the class into small groups and gives them the instructions shown in Figure 4.10. The instructor should assign each group one of the following cultural metaphors: the Swedish Stuga, the German Symphony, the Italian Opera, or the Chinese Family Altar (for Taiwan). A specific metaphor can be assigned to more than one group.

The instructor should also give each group an overhead on which to write its slogan. Time limit for working in the group is 10 minutes.

EXERCISE 4.10   Creating a Complete Advertisement

This exercise extends the learning provided by Exercise 4.9 and builds upon it. Students are again assigned to small groups, and each group is assigned a cultural metaphor. However, the instructions are now expanded to include other approaches, namely Hofstede's and Hall's approaches plus the specific cultural metaphor. Also, the goal is to create a full advertisement, which may or may not include the advertising slogan created in Exercise 4.9.

Students should work in their groups for about 20 to 30 minutes. Each group prepares one or two overheads for class presentation.

It is important to stress that the students should incorporate the cultural knowledge they have been studying, and that they should avoid broad-based stereotypes (see Figure 4.11).

It is particularly helpful if at least two groups independently develop an advertisement for the same nation, because the students can then compare and contrast them. Also, the instructor should point out how useful cultural knowledge can be, particularly cultural metaphors. For example, to attract both Swedes and Italians to the Southwest, Native American reservations can be highlighted, but Native American ceremonies should probably be stressed more for the Italians than for the Swedes because of the subcategories of pageantry and spectacle, voice, and exteriority in Italian culture.

As indicated above, each group is encouraged to use the specific cultural metaphor, its categories, and Hofstede's dimensions in developing their plans. It is also possible to have one group use only Hofstede's dimensions. Another alternative is to have all groups work on one nation, or have two or more groups work on the same nation. Finally, the instructor may want to use this exercise in conjunction with Exercise 6.5, Mangled Advertising Campaigns, or possibly just the overhead for this exercise, Figure 6.1.

FIGURE 4.9. Characteristics of the Metaphors

Swedish Stuga

■ Love of untrammeled nature

■ Individualism through self-development

■ Equality

American Football

■ Tailgate party

■ Individualism and competitive specialization

■ Complex plays (playbook)

■ Unpredictable outcomes, high risk, aggressive (violent), rich rewards

■ Huddling—people from different backgrounds and abilities come together periodically to solve short-term problems. Football is the only game in the world having a huddle after every play. Teamwork + competitive specialization

■ Ceremonial celebration of perfection

German Symphony

■ Focus on enduring achievement

■ Precision and synchronicity

■ Subordination of individual goals to group goals

Italian Opera

■ Operatic overture

■ Pageantry and spectacle

■ Voice or lyrical quality. More vowels than consonants. Talking = singing

■ Exteriority. The belief that the individual cannot keep thoughts and emotions to himself or herself. Thoughts and emotions must be expressed, first in the family and then in the piazza. Equivalent to the crowd scenes in opera

■ Interaction between soloists and chorus, similar to the interaction between the individual and the group, and between regional identity (north or south) and national identity

Chinese Family Altar (for Taiwan)

■ Harmony within the family and, if possible, outside of it

■ Capacity to change while maintaining solid traditions

■ Well-integrated social unit uniting generations, including the dead, who are still considered to be present

FIGURE 4.10. Instructions for the Advertising Slogan Exercise

- Your team has been hired by the largest U.S. travel agency to attract people from other nations to the United States.

- You need to develop an advertising slogan to enhance the possibility that people from the nation assigned to your group will travel to the United States. This slogan cannot be more than 100 words. Assume that you will be presenting your slogan to the top management team of this travel agency. You must be creative but logical and convincing. Also, you must use the cultural knowledge that you possess to construct your slogan.

- Your slogan should overlap the cultural metaphors of the United States and your selected nation, but not totally. People must feel comfortable (overlap), but the slogan should include activities not available at home.

- Avoid broad-gauged stereotypes.

FIGURE 4.11. Instructions for Creating a Complete Advertisement

- Your team has been hired by the largest U.S. travel agency to attract people from other nations to the United States.

- You need to develop an advertisement to motivate people from your assigned nation to travel to the United States. Assume that you will be presenting your advertisement to the top management team of this travel agency. You must be creative but logical and convincing. Also, you must use the cultural knowledge you have obtained in this class to construct your advertisement.

- Based on Hofstede's dimensions, the cultural metaphor for your nation, and the characteristics of this metaphor, which places in the United States would be attractive?

- Which features of the area(s) selected would you highlight?

- Remember, your advertisement should overlay the cultural metaphors of the United States and your selected nation, but not totally. People must feel comfortable (overlap), but the advertisement should include activities not available at home.

- Avoid broad-gauged stereotypes.

■ **COMMENTS**

Marketing and advertising are particularly appropriate for cross-cultural exercises, because the teacher can go over well-known fiascos such as trying to sell the Nova automobile in Spain, where the literal translation is "no go"; selling perfume in India in a bottle with a cap that looked like the head of Buddha; and making Nike shoes that had a representation of Allah on them. Also, the teacher can point out that there are significant differences in consumer preferences around the world, although there are also similarities, thus reinforcing the overlap between cultural metaphors. Importantly, the exercise is structured in such a way that the student does not need any background in marketing or advertising, although it would be helpful.

▍ USING METAPHORS TO COMPARE GOVERNMENT AND BUSINESS

Co-Determination in Germany Versus Single Determination in the United States

The instructor should briefly review the cultural metaphors for Germany and the United States (see Figure 4.9). He or she should then describe the unique system of co-determination in Germany, with its two boards, and compare it to the single board of directors in the United States.

The instructor should point out that Germany emphasizes social democracy, or a system in which economic competition is limited to some extent in order to protect as many citizens as possible. Co-determination is a major mechanism of social democracy. Basically, each company has a dual board, unlike the situation in the United States, where there is only one board of directors per company. The two board types are supervisory (*Aufsichtsrat*) and management (*Vorstand*). Supervisory board members include large shareholders, some employees, and some labor union representatives. The two boards must work together on goals and company objectives. Also, a company must have a separate workers' council (*Betriebsrat*), which has the right to monitor all corporate plans and actions.

For example, a downsizing plan must be agreed upon by members of the Vorstand, then approved by the Aufsichtsrat, and, finally, presented to the Betriebsrat before the powerful national unions have the opportunity to review the plan.

EXERCISE 4.11	The German Symphony, American Football, and Boards of Directors

Using think-pair-share, the instructor should ask the students to examine these organizational arrangements in terms of these cultural metaphors. The instructor can also refer to Hofstede's rankings of the United States and Germany on five cross-cultural dimensions (see Figure 3.1).

Company Mergers in Germany and the United States

Research has consistently indicated that 7 or 8 out of every 10 joint activities between firms, such as joint ventures and mergers, prove to be very problematic. The instructor can point out three major reasons why such activities continue, which are as follows:

- Companies possess nonoverlapping core competencies that theoretically strengthen the new organizational arrangement. A core competence is an internal strength and/or resource that is difficult to imitate, valuable, rare, and nonsubstitutable (e.g., Wal-Mart's logistic system).
- Companies have the early mover advantage, especially in the international area.
- Companies have increasing market share and visibility.

EXERCISE 4.12	Applying the German Symphony and American Football to Mergers of Companies

The instructor can divide the class into small groups. Each group should be assigned one of the mergers below. The group should research this merger and apply cultural knowledge to it, focusing specifically on the cross-cultural issues. These German-American mergers are as follows:

- DaimlerChrysler
- Deutsche Bank and Bankers Trust

Each group can prepare a class presentation using overheads and/or write a five-page paper.

Cultural Differences in Other Business Settings

EXERCISE 4.13 — Managerial Interviews, Joint Ventures, and Cultural Metaphors

Several instructors have used two or more cultural metaphors to analyze an international venture through interviews with managers. Students can work independently or in small groups. They read about a particular international alliance, such as DaimlerChrysler, and create an interview that incorporates economic-focused questions and culturally focused questions derived from the cultural metaphors. Each student or group then writes a paper summarizing the interview data. Class presentations can also be scheduled.

EXERCISE 4.14 — Selling Furniture

The instructor should break students into small groups. Have them assume the role of sales associates at a furniture store. This store has a diverse customer base. If you were selling furniture to customers of different ethnic backgrounds, how would you tailor your approach? Using the cultural metaphor model (e.g., see Figure 4.9), describe what type of furniture you would likely sell to a customer who is

- Spanish
- German
- Italian
- Swedish
- Indian
- English

Alternatively, the instructor can use the think-pair-share method with the entire class and focus on one nation and its cultural metaphor, or one nation at a time.

EXERCISE 4.15   Office Assignments

The instructor should divide the class into small groups. Each group should be assigned one cultural metaphor (e.g., see Figure 4.9). The group should then describe how the following case about office assignments would be generally solved in each nation. The case is taken from Gannon (1988).

Office assignments are very important in an organization. When desirable offices become available, individuals frequently struggle to obtain them. But large-scale reassignments of offices tend to create uneasiness and uncertainty. Individuals perceive, sometimes correctly, that an assignment to a less desirable office is akin to a demotion and a strong indication that top management is unhappy with their work.

In a College of Business Administration of 60 faculty members within a large university, 20 additional offices became available when the sociology department moved to a new building. Thus, it was not possible for every faculty member to move into a more desirable office, but certainly some of them would be able to do so. Immediately, however, problems emerged. Some faculty members with many years of service felt that they deserved priority in office assignments, especially if they were full professors (the three tenure-track ranks in this university were Professor, tenured Associate Professors, and untenured Assistant Professor). However, some younger faculty members with outstanding publication records did not agree with this stance. They felt that offices should be assigned to the best performers, regardless of rank or seniority.

To compound the problem, there was much disagreement about the measurement of outstanding performance. Should it be measured in terms of teaching; scholarly publications in journals emphasizing statistical testing of hypotheses; publications in more popular and widely distributed periodicals such as *Business Week* and *The Harvard Business Review*; or university, professional, and community service?

The Executive Committee of the College was responsible for making this decision on reallocation of offices. It consisted of the Associate Dean for Academic Affairs and the six chairpersons of the six faculty groups (Accounting, Finance, Marketing, Management Science and Statistics, Management and Organization, and General Business).

The instructor can then point out that it took this Executive Committee 3 months to come up with a satisfactory solution, which reflects both good decision making and American pragmatism. The solution was as follows:

- To be eligible for a new office, a faculty member had to give up the right to his or her current office.

- A pool of offices was then created consisting of the new offices and the offices put into the pool by faculty members.

- The Executive Committee used the method of paired comparison to rank order the 25 faculty members being considered for a change in office. This rank ordering was based purely on overall performance in the three areas of research, teaching, and service.

- The Committee then created six performance groups within this rank ordering. Within each performance group, seniority was used as the basis for assigning offices.

EXERCISE 4.16   Analyzing Advertisements

Exercises 4.9 and 4.10 emphasized creating advertisements using cultural metaphors. This exercise asks that the students or trainees examine the two ads in Figure 4.12, one of which was created for the Hispanic American culture and the other for the White Anglo-Saxon culture. The instructor should ask: What is the major difference between these two ads?

Research has suggested that the Spanish culture is more responsive to emotional appeals than the Anglo-Saxon culture, which is more responsive to factual details. This research is consistent with the cultural metaphors of the Spanish Bullfight and American Football (see Gannon & Associates, in press). The instructor may want to point out that southern European nations tend to be more emotionally expressive than northern European nations (e.g., see the German Symphony and Italian Opera in Gannon & Associates, in press).

EXERCISE 4.17   Military and Business Strategy

A well-known exercise in business strategy is comparing French and German strategies in the fight of Paris in 1914 during World War I. Students usually read excerpts from Barbara Tuchman's *The Guns of August,* reprinted in pages 129-143 of Henry Mintzberg and James Brian Quinn's *The Strategy Process: Context and Cases.*

Have small groups read the metaphor for France (French Wine) and also the metaphor for Germany (the German Symphony) and apply these cultural metaphors to the respective strategies.

EXERCISE 4.18   International Strategies

Using the Harvard Business School's Web site or another source, select an international strategy case that is country specific. Then, have small groups apply the cultural metaphor of that nation to the analysis of the case. In addition to coming up with general business-level strategy, have students also integrate cultural metaphors to support their recommended strategy.

FIGURE 4.12.

Informational Ad: Coat

This winter, come to Rex Coats to find the greatest variety of styles and fabrics in all kinds of coats.

Since the beginning of the century, we have been providing customers with winter apparel. Because the manufacturers at Rex Coats use only materials that have been clinically proven to preserve heat, our coats provide protection against any kind of weather.

Our product is made of nonsynthetic liners, which create its characteristic comfort. And we assure you that our prices are the lowest in the market.

We have a great variety of styles, both casual and dressy, as well as a great selection of materials, such as leather, corduroy, nylon, and wool.

Come visit us today. The staff at Rex Coats is knowledgeable and ready to provide customers with any information about our products.

Emotional Ad: Coat

Feel warm and look cool with Rex Coats!

Since we first opened our doors, we have been helping people find just what they need to face the winter. This winter, you can count on Rex Coats to make you feel cozy and warm. Our fabrics are so soft that they will feel like velvet on your skin!

Just imagine! Whether going to work, on a night out, or playing sports, you will feel great in a Rex Coat. Our prices are so good that you'll have to look twice to believe it!

Because we want you to find the style that is just right for you, we offer you a wide range of choices from which you can pick just what suits you.

Come visit us today! Each member of our staff is committed to you and will help you find a coat that you will feel great about.

SOURCE: France (1999).

EXERCISE 4.19   Organization Design and Work Groups

The instructor should point out that there are several differences between the United States, with its emphasis on individualism, and Japan, with its emphasis on collectivism. A good example is the free-rider effect, or social loafing, in the United States: When working in groups, some individuals tend to loaf or not do their proportionate share of the work. However, in collectivistic nations such as Japan, individuals tend to work harder in the group because of the sense of group solidarity and responsibility.

This exercise was developed by Michele Gelfand. It employs both cultural metaphors and a good understanding of the research on cross-cultural work groups, particularly in the United States and Japan. As background reading, the instructor should assign "The Japanese Garden" from Gannon and Associates (2001). He or she must also assign "The Japanese Work Group" (Kashima & Callan, 1994). Gannon and Associates use the Japanese Garden as a cultural metaphor, which is supplemented by Kashima and Callan's use of the Japanese IE or Japanese Household.

This exercise involves adopting American management practices in Japan and Japanese management practices in the United States. The instructor should emphasize that practices taken from one culture into another culture must be tailored to the culture and not transported wholesale.

The instructor should assign trainees or students to one of two groups: consultants to Nikkon or consultants to Ameritech. The Nikkon consultants have been hired by Nikkon, a large Japanese manufacturing company, because this company is considering the use of American practices in its Japanese-based operations in the areas of compensation, performance evaluation, job tenure, and so on. The instructor should assign about five trainees to a group. He or she does not need to assign everyone to a group; other class members can serve as the company's board of directors, to whom the consultants present their analysis.

The Nikkon consultants and Ameritech consultants, who consist of both native-born Japanese and native-born Americans, are considered to be experts on both Japan and the United States. The Nikkon consultants should receive the following instructions:

- Describe the nature and structure of the organization and groups in the United States and Japan, using the notion of vertical and horizontal roles, that is, Triandis's two types of individualism and two types of collectivism (see Chapter 3 and Kashima & Callan, 1994). Describe how these roles are consistent with the larger sociocultural context, that is, the rankings of the United States and Japan on Hofstede's dimensions. Also describe the adequacy of these roles for preparing individuals for new organizational experiences and changes. In other words, compare and contrast in your analysis.

- Highlight reasons why it could be productive for Nikkon to make changes in their system. Note deficiencies of the current system, economic and related changes influencing Japan, and so on.

■ Also describe major aspects of the American system that you feel would lead to better results than the current Japanese system in operation. Be specific in your recommendations. Be sure to indicate how general practices could be tailored specifically to the Japanese context. In other words, indicate the specific changes you would recommend if Nikkon wants to adopt American practices, keeping in mind the importance of fit or congruence with the larger culture.

■ Describe aspects of the U.S. work system that should not be adopted at all, given their incongruity in the Japanese cultural context. Also describe the aspects of the current system (at Nikkon) that you would not recommend changing.

The instructions to the Ameritech consultants would be very similar, except that Ameritech is an American-based manufacturing company that is considering the use of Japanese management practices. A natural dialogue and spirited discussion should develop in the classroom setting as the consultants present their analyses to the boards of the two companies. However, for this exercise to work well, the trainees must do the background reading. The objective of this exercise is to show the links between cultural metaphors, research, and practical implications in the area of managing work groups effectively.

CHAPTER 5

Cultures as Processes, Outcomes, and Emotional Expression

Edward Hall (Hall & Hall, 1990) is a prominent cultural anthropologist whose work on monochronic and polychronic time is highlighted in Chapter 2. His theoretical framework also includes a concept known as the context of culture or communication. Basically, Hall argued that there is a continuum extending from a low to high degree of intense socialization within cultural groups. According to Hall, low socialization requires a culture in which information must be transmitted orally and/or in written form; otherwise, members do not know what to do. High socialization indicates that messages are transmitted subtly, because everyone knows what to do. For example, one Japanese saying is "Silence is communication," which means that group members know what to do based on the length of each silence. Although the same amount of meaning can be conveyed in a low-socialized or low-context culture as in a high-socialized or high-context culture, the means would be different. Germany and the United States stand at the low end of Hall's context dimension, whereas Japan and Saudi Arabia are on the other end.

Gannon and Associates (1994) have argued that high-context cultures, which tend to be more collectivistic than individualistic, are very concerned about the processes of interactions and communications. They want to know an outsider before doing business with him or her. Such cultures are also concerned about outcomes, but effective and smooth interactional and communication processes must be in place before outcomes for both parties can be considered.

Also, Gannon has argued that socialization is emphasized in process-oriented and outcome-oriented cultures, for example, the emphasis on religion in both situations. But outcome-focused individuals tend to deemphasize processes preceding a discussion of mutual outcomes.

Using these concepts, Gannon has proposed a four-fold typology of national cultures. The two dimensions defining these national cultures are the degree to which processes are emphasized before outcomes can be considered, and the degree of emotional expressiveness (see Figure 5.1).

EXERCISE 5.1   **Seeing Processes, Outcomes, and Emotional Expression in Action**

Chapter 8 describes films and cross-cultural videos that an instructor can employ. I have found that a few videos are extremely effective in highlighting the concept of context and the fourfold typology of national cultures emphasizing processes, outcomes, and emotional expressiveness. Typically, I ask the trainees or students to observe short video segments and to interpret them using cultural metaphors, the perspectives of both Hall and Hofstede, and the fourfold typology of national cultures. Additional information on obtaining these videos is provided in Chapter 8.

■ COMMENTS

Going International, Part 2 contains a sequence in which an American interacts with a Saudi ruler. The American wants to achieve an outcome and is oblivious to processes, even to the extent that he commits serious cultural blunders, such as handing papers with his left hand, asking about the ruler's wife, and so on. Typically, trainees can identify these "dos and taboos," but they need to look closely for processes. For instance, the ruler behaves polychronically, and he is very sensitive to the input from the other Saudis in the room. After discussing this video segment, the instructor can show the video evaluation of it by the experts, who tend to focus only on dos and taboos.

A second video segment involves a Mexican and an American businessman. This segment highlights the importance of processes and emotional expressiveness. After discussing the segment, the instructor should show the evaluation by experts, as the Mexican gets the last laugh, literally speaking.

A newer video similar to the above is *Work Today*. Like its predecessor, it includes several short interactions that can be interpreted using Hofstede, Hall, cultural metaphors, and the fourfold typology.

West Meets East in Japan contains a short segment on business cards followed by a segment on the difficulty of saying no in some cultures. Again, these segments are wonderful for highlighting the theoretical perspectives and also the dos and taboos.

FIGURE 5.1.

FIGURE 5.1.

OPEN EXPRESSION OF EMOTIONS AND FEELINGS

	Lower	Higher
Lower	England, Ireland, and Scotland	United States
Higher	China, Japan, and India	Mexico, Spain, and Italy

DEGREE TO WHICH PROCESS MUST BE EMPHASIZED BEFORE OUTCOMES CAN BE

73

Finally, *Cross-Talk, Part 2: Performance Appraisal Across Cultures* contains a series of goal-setting interviews based on actual interviews conducted at the Bank of America. Both interviewers and interviewees are females in all instances, but their cultural backgrounds are Anglo American, Chinese American, and Korean American. Some differences are obvious, for example, the Chinese American and Korean American keep emphasizing facts but not conclusions. Also, when the Anglo interviewer asks the Anglo interviewee how well she did in meeting her goals, the interviewee responded as most Americans would: "I did great." This is the beginning of a dialogue.

However, the Chinese and Korean Americans never state a conclusion. In high-context or process-oriented cultures, the conclusion is typically not stated first and then defended and amended through dialog. Rather, such cultures stress the communication of facts of the *situation,* from which the conclusion should be obvious to the leader.

The notes accompanying this video point out an interesting study in which Chinese managers who speak perfect English listened to an audiotape on which American managers were making decisions. The Chinese thought that the Americans were crazy. The Americans felt the same way when they listened to the Chinese managers making decisions.

EXERCISE 5.2   Southern Versus Northern Hospitality

The instructor can point out that Hall's framework and the fourfold typology of culture can be applied to many situations, both within one nation and across nations. For example, Hispanic Americans tend to be more emotionally expressive than Anglo Americans. The instructor should read the following critical incident and ask the students to interpret it using the context dimension and the fourfold typology. Think-pair-share should be employed. After the discussion, the instructor can ask the students to provide similar experiences.

CASE STUDY

Charlie, a former professor from Yazoo, Mississippi, had come to visit a boyhood friend in New York City. The friend was working with IBM and was married. Charlie was just admitted to Columbia University, where he eventually became a professor. Around 9 p.m., Charlie said, almost without thinking, that he thought it was time for him to go. In Mississippi, the host would strongly argue that it was too early, that they had time for another drink or two, and so on. Around midnight, the guest would be expected to leave, even though the host was still suggesting that he stay, and he would finally leave, with regrets being expressed on all sides.

However, in New York City, his boyhood friend said, "Yes, I think it is time." All of a sudden, Charlie found himself out in the snow, and, as he said, he was never so surprised in all of his life.

EXERCISE 5.3　　The Hong Kong Orchestra

The instructor should read aloud the following case study and s[...]
ask specific questions, which are in parentheses.

It seemed like such a small problem. Ed, a 24-year-old American who ha[...] the Hong Kong Orchestra as second violin, worked well with Tad, a 35-year-old F[...] who was the first violin, until Tad began to come late to practices or missed them completely. A symphonic orchestra demands some direction from the leader of each of its sections, and Tad started to become ineffective in this capacity because of his tardiness and absences.

At first only mildly annoyed, Ed began to assume the leadership of the violin section by default, but inevitably, the section's performance began to decline. Ed expressed his annoyance to Tad in rather mild terms, at least from an American perspective. Tad simply did not respond in any way, not even responding directly to Ed's statements. *(Instructor should ask: What should Ed do?)*

Finally, Ed showed his annoyance at one rehearsal when the violin section was doing poorly, telling Tad—in a sufficiently loud manner so that a few other orchestra members heard him—that the violin section's performance had deteriorated because of his repeated tardiness and absence, that he needed to show some leadership, and that Tad was burdening him with work that was properly his own. *(How do you think Tad responded? Why?)* Tad did not even look at him or acknowledge his presence or statement. *(What should Ed do now?)*

Visibly upset, Ed approached William, the manager of the orchestra, and asked that he, William, and Tad get together to "iron things out directly." However, William was experienced at cross-cultural interactions and knew that Tad had suffered a loss of face, which is the unwritten set of rules that individuals and groups use to ensure individual dignity and group harmony. William did set up a meeting. *(Who do you think William invited to this meeting?)* The meeting included Min, a translator of Tagalog (a major Filipino dialect), even though Tad spoke English fluently; Ed; Tad; John, the orchestra's conductor; and William himself. William wanted to solve this problem but, at the same time, make everyone feel satisfied and ensure that face was safeguarded.

(How should William arrange the seating at this meeting? Why? How should communication be allowed to occur at this meeting? For example, should William take charge of the interactions, and if so, in what way? How specific should the resulting action plan be? Based on your answers to these questions, what do you think happened after this meeting occurred?)

In the meeting, William sat behind his desk, with Tad to his extreme left, then Min, then John, and then Ed at the extreme right. William controlled the communication process by talking first to Min, who translated into Tagalog for Tad; then to Ed; then to John, and so on. Everyone communicated only with and through William. At the end of the meeting, Tad did agree to change his behavior, and Ed promised to have no more emotional outbursts. Hence, face was preserved.

However, Tad completely avoided communicating with Ed as much as possible. Ed became so miserable that he quit after a few months. Eight years later, Ed still spoke emotionally about how badly he had acted. But he was lucky. Many times, an individual will make a major cross-cultural mistake and no one will tell him. At least Ed could change his future behavior.

This case study is an excellent illustration of problems that can occur between low-context and high-context individuals and cultures. (This case is adapted from Gannon & Associates, 1994.)

EXERCISE 5.4 — Problem-Solving Approaches

This exercise is based on a case study involving two friends with different cultural backgrounds:

CASE STUDY

It seemed like such a small problem. Ed, a 24-year-old American who had recently joined the Hong Kong Orchestra as second violin, worked well with Tad, a 35-year-old Filipino who was the first violin, until Tad began to come late to practices or missed them completely. A symphonic orchestra demands some direction from the leader of each of its sections, and Tad started to become ineffective in this capacity because of his tardiness and absences.

At first only mildly annoyed, Ed began to assume the leadership of the violin section by default, but inevitably, the section's performance began to decline. Ed expressed his annoyance to Tad in rather mild terms, at least from an American perspective. Tad simply did not respond in any way, not even responding directly to Ed's statements. *(Instructor should ask: What should Ed do?)*

The instructor can ask, Which approach do you favor? Why? Which is more low context? If you decide to confront Joe, what would you say, and how would you say it?

EXERCISE 5.5 — Religions and Cultures

In training large numbers of students and managers, I have found that a very large number of them want to learn more about how religion relates to culture. In Gannon and Associates (1994, 2001), I deliberately tried to relate cultural metaphors to religions. See the discussion of Islam in "The Turkish Coffeehouse," Buddhism in "The Japanese Garden," Confucianism and Taoism in "The Chinese Family Altar," and Hinduism in "The Dance of Shiva." I use the charts (Figures 5.2, 5.3, 5.4, and 5.5) to explain the basic concepts of each religion and then relate them to the cultural metaphors. I have found that the material can be covered in about 30 minutes of lecture accompanied by some discussion, but frequently, the discussion increases the amount of time. The instructor can use these charts or adapt them to his or her needs. If you want additional background, Smith's *The World's Religions* (1991) is splendid.

FIGURE 5.2. Buddhism

Basic concepts:

- Reaction to the excesses of Hinduism

- The four noble truths: Life is suffering (*Dukkha*); the cause is self-centered desire (*Tanha*); there is a solution; this is the eightfold path (right outlook, intent, speech, conduct, livelihood, effort, mindful-ness, and concentration)

- Right conduct: Do not kill, steal, lie, be unchaste, or drink (Buddhist version of the second or ethical half of the Ten Commandments)

- Basic ideas are also a part of Hinduism (e.g., karma, migration of souls both upward and downward, and *mukti* or liberation)

- Practice moderation in all things, including emotional expression

- Two general types of Buddhism: Big Raft (meditation and helping others) and Little Raft (primarily medita-tion or inward-focused)

NOTE: For a discussion of religions, see Smith (1991).

FIGURE 5.3. Confucianism

Background:

- A reaction to the turmoil in 6th-century China
- No concept of a personal God with attributes
- Netherworld from which ancestors advise the living
- Emphasis on rituals leading to the good family and life
- Focused on the practical and this world

Key concepts:

- *Jen,* or human heartedness
- *Chuntzu,* or the Superior Man who helps others
- *Li,* or the way things should be accomplished through rituals and the five major relationships: father and son; older and younger siblings; husband and wife; older and younger friend; and ruler and subject
- *Te,* or ruling others by moral example
- Roundness, or the family as a well-knit integrated unit, including ancestors
- Harmony, especially in the family
- Fluidity, or the capacity to change while honoring traditions

Taoism:

- Mystical religion representing the rhythm and driving force of nature
- Yin and yang or no clear dichotomies
- Against violence

NOTE: See "The Chinese Family Altar," in Gannon and Associates (1994, 2001).

FIGURE 5.4. Hinduism

Key concepts:

- An emphasis on the cyclicality of existence and numerous gods

- Cyclicality is expressed in the Hindu Trinity: Brahma (creator), Vishnu (preserver), and Shiva (destroyer)

- Wants of humans (Maslow's hierarchy)

- Transmigration of souls, up and down

- Karma: Our existence or soul is the consequence of our actions

- Existence we know is illusory

- Four ways to achieve salvation (*mukti*)

Different cycles:

- Life (different stages)

- Family

- Social interaction (drama or duty)

- Work and rejuvenation

- Relationships (e.g., bargaining)

NOTE: See "India: The Dance of Shiva," in Gannon and Associates (1994, in press).

FIGURE 5.5. Islam

The Five Pillars of Islam:

- There is no God but Allah, and Mohammed is his prophet.

- Submit to God's will (e.g., pray five times daily).

- Observe Ramadan for one month and fast during daylight hours.

- Give to charity (10% of income).

- Make one trip to Mecca.

Other important facts:

- Mohammed viewed Judaism and Christianity as earlier forms of religion leading to Islam.

- Similar to Confucianism, Islam arose during a period of social upheaval.

- Islamic nations, with the exception of Turkey, are theocracies.

- The Koran is viewed as the repository of the basic beliefs that Muslims should follow.

NOTE: See "The Turkish Coffeehouse," in Gannon and Associates (1994, 2001).

CHAPTER 6

Sociolinguistics

It is frequently asserted that approximately 30% of the communication between individuals is transmitted by the words they use. The other 70% occurs through the following types of nonverbal communication:

- Kinetics—the study of body movements

- Proxemics—the study of personal and social space

- Paralanguage—the study of how things are said

These areas fall under the general classification of sociolinguistics, or the dynamic interaction between language and the social environment within which the communication process occurs. In this chapter, we focus specifically on sociolinguistics.

EXERCISE 6.1   Words, Phrases, and Cultural Meanings

The instructor can use the think-pair-share method for this exercise.

There are some words that seem to capture the essence of a culture but cannot be translated accurately. For example, "Mai pen rai" in Thai roughly translates to "Things happen such as the electricity going out; you have little, if any, control over such things; so don't worry about them, and sit back and relax." This phrase captures a large part of the essence of Thai culture. Can you think of other words and phrases in a specific culture or cultures that capture essential cultural meanings but are very difficult to translate?

EXERCISE 6.2   **Colors and Cultural Meanings**

Do colors have any cultural meaning? Some colors seem to convey the feelings and beliefs of a culture. For example, red, white, and blue seem to effectively convey the positive and patriotic feelings of the American culture. Also, the color blue in China represents death or a funeral, whereas red is a very positive color.

   The instructor can use the think-pair-share method. Can the students or trainees think of any other colors that have cultural meaning?

■ COMMENTS

   After the student input, the instructor can indicate that colors often convey very effectively the feeling of culture. Green easily conveys the thought of a shamrock and the Irish culture. Sometimes, the same color can convey thoughts about more than one culture, such as the red of Japan's rising sun and of Canada's maple leaf. Colors also can come to represent subgroups within culture. Similarly, teams use colors to distinguish themselves, and the color of the team becomes inseparable from the accomplishments and pride in that team.

EXERCISE 6.3   **The Deaf Culture**

The deaf culture has unique aspects that can often transcend an individual's national culture. For example, the deaf typically will have conversations face to face, which helps to strengthen and deepen the relationships they form with individuals with whom they communicate. If two deaf acquaintances are walking toward each other, they will typically stop and have a face-to-face conversation. This is in contrast to the abrupt greeting in passing that most hearing individuals tend to have.

   The instructor can ask the class to use Kluckholn's six dimensions of culture to profile the deaf community. This exercise can occur in small groups or using the think-pair-share method.

■ COMMENTS

   The instructor can point out that deaf individuals do not see themselves as handicapped. Rather, they believe that they have a unique culture that is merely different from that of the hearing world. Part of this culture is rooted in the idea of the relationship. In contrast to those with normal hearing, the deaf must generally communicate in close proximity; thus, they build stronger relationships with those with whom they communicate.

The deaf tend to experience time uniquely. In contrast to those with normal hearing, time is drawn out. Everything seems longer.

The instructor may point out at least one controversy. The deaf culture is so strong that many of the deaf do not like other deaf people to associate too much with those possessing normal hearing. Such behavior is frequently considered to be crazy, and the deaf will make gestures signifying such meaning when discussing deaf people who devote too much time with individuals having normal hearing.

This controversy has been heightened in recent years because of the creation of hearing devices that allow many of the deaf to hear quite well, if not as well as those with normal hearing. Some deaf groups oppose the use of such devices because of their belief in the uniqueness of the deaf culture. Other deaf groups, however, view these hearing devices as a way into a normal life similar to that experienced by those with normal hearing.

EXERCISE 6.4 Stereotyping National Cultures

The instructor can employ the think-pair-share method. He should ask the students or trainees to identify the five adjectives that are most descriptive of Americans, and the five adjectives that are least descriptive of Americans. He can then report a study published in *Newsweek* (July 11, 1983, p. 50) that used this exercise in six nations: the Unitd States, France, Japan, Germany, Britain, and Brazil. In four of the six nations, the following adjectives were put forth as most descriptive of Americans: industrious, energetic, inventive, and friendly. All six nations felt that the adjective "lazy" was least descriptive of Americans, and three of the six nations also selected "crude" and "honest."

The instructor can compare the class profiles to the results of this survey and, if differences exist, probe as to why.

EXERCISE 6.5 Mangled Advertising Campaigns

The instructor should divide the class into small groups. Each group should try to describe a particularly successful advertising campaign or campaigns, and the group members think the campaign was a success.. Then, each group should try to describe a culturally insensitive advertising campaign or campaigns. As an alternative, the instructor can use the think-pair-share method with the entire class, focusing on a successful campaign(s) and/or a culturally insensitive campaign(s). The instructor can then use Figure 6.1 as an overhead.

FIGURE 6.1. Mangled Translations: Real Advertising Slogans

- Kentucky Fried Chicken in China: The "finger lickin' good" slogan translates as "Eat your fingers off."

- Pepsi in Taiwan. The translation of the slogan "The Pepsi Generation" came out to "Pepsi will bring your ancestors back from the dead."

- Salem cigarettes in Japan. The slogan "Salem—Feeling Free" translates as "When smoking Salem, you feel so refreshed that your mind seems to be free and empty."

- Ford in Brazil. When the Pinto flopped, the company found out that the slogan translated as "tiny male genitals."

- Chevy in Mexico. Sales of the Nova may have been affected by the fact that in Spanish, its literal translation is "no go."

- Purdue Chicken in Mexico. His slogan "It takes a tough man to make a tender chicken" may have worked well in the United States, but it shocked people in Mexico because the literal translation can also mean "It takes a hard man to make a chicken aroused."

- One airline advertised, after translation, "We take your bags and send them in all directions."

EXERCISE 6.6   Nonverbal Communication

The instructor can demonstrate the importance of nonverbal communication by selecting a student volunteer to come to the front of the classroom. Then, the instructor should violate his or her need for personal space by moving very close to the volunteer, even to the point of being eye-to-eye and gesturing dramatically. Ordinarily, the student—particularly those students from northern Europe and similar places—will keep backing up to avoid contact. The instructor can reiterate the importance of personal space (see Exercises 2.7 and 2.8) and focus on nonverbal communication (e.g., eye contact, gestures, etc.).

Alternatively, the instructor can use think-pair-share. He or she can ask the class for examples of pleasant or unpleasant experiences involving body movements, hand and arm gestures, violations of personal space, and so on.

EXERCISE 6.7   Just Say No

The instructor can point out that different cultures have different ways of saying no. For example, low-context Americans frequently do not hide their feelings and just say no as soon as their minds are made up. However, the high-context Japanese tend to say "maybe" or "that would be difficult," which is equivalent to the American no.

The instructor should use the think-pair-share method and, after giving the example above, ask for examples from other cultures.

Afterwards, the instructor can cite as examples the high-context Thais, who tend to change the subject; Nigerians and others who, to be polite, will not say no to a party invitation but will simply not show up; and the Chinese, whose phrase "mei guanxi" literally translates as "it doesn't matter," but its underlying meaning is "no relationship," something that is fundamental to the Chinese.

EXERCISE 6.8   Global Virtual Teams

In this exercise, students imagine that they have been put in charge of a project involving management from Taiwan, the United States, Germany, and Brazil. These are all very successful managers with high self-confidence and large egos. Moreover, although the project is very important, the manager has only 2 months to complete it, and all interactions must be made via telephone and computer. There will be no face-to-face meetings.

The instructor should have the class break into small groups. Each group should design a cross-cultural training program to take place on the Internet before the work begins. The program should last 3 hours. Remember that these managers have never met face to face, although they work for the same company. Use Hofstede's dimensions, Hall's revised context of culture, the fourfold model of culture, cultural metaphors, and sociolinguistics.

EXERCISE 6.9   Interviews About Languages

Experts agree that the number of languages is declining. Perhaps there are only 4,000 distinct languages, when there were at one time as many as 10,000, although the number of major language groups seems to be stable. There is even a group of linguistic anthropologists that is holding conferences on language death.

Conversely, there are some old languages that are being revived in Europe. For example, as a counterreaction to European centralization, there are many regional cultures trying to revitalize their roots. One such example is a family in France whose parents have taught their children how to speak Breton—an almost Welsh language—that their ancestors spoke. Similarly, Catalonia in Spain and Wales in the United Kingdom are becoming more region-centric than Eurocentric these days.

The instructor should require each student who speaks only English to interview a student who speaks multiple languages. If only a few students are fluent in more than one language, then use a larger group setting. Have the students speaking only English ask the others about their feelings on the issue. Do they feel comfortable switching from one language to another language? Do they feel more self-confident because they know more than one language?

■ COMMENTS

Afterwards, the instructor should point out that individuals switching easily from one language to another significantly change their mental and emotional frameworks. For example, one Spanish woman married to a northern European tended to be quiet and reserved in that setting. However, her entire personality changed when communicating with Spanish people, even over the phone. She became extroverted and loquacious. Her husband was dumbfounded when he first saw this transformation.

EXERCISE 6.10

The Language of Gestures

There are different languages of gestures in different nations and ethnic groups that symbolically convey meaning (Ekman, Friesen, & Bear, 1984). What is a positive gesture in one nation may be a negative gesture elsewhere. The instructor can ask: What meaning is attached to the thumb-and-forefinger-in-a-circle gesture? Students tend to see this gesture as friendly, indicating that you are "OK." But in France and Belgium, this means "You're a zero."

Similarly, the gesture in which the index finger points to a person's temple when the other fingers are curved indicates in the United States that a person is intelligent. In Europe, however, this gesture indicates that the person is stupid. However, the verbal context determines how this gesture is interpreted, positively or negatively.

Using think-pair-share, the instructor should ask the students to identify gestures having different meanings in different places.

CHAPTER 7

Additional Behaviors
Across Cultures

In this chapter, we provide exercises for additional behaviors that are significant across cultures. These behaviors are related to the concepts presented in previous chapters, such as individualism and collectivism.

As background for the exercises in this chapter, the instructor should present the following empirical "facts" in a rather definitive manner, emphasizing that these "facts" are supported by incomplete data. First, social class is more influential in explaining values, attitudes, and behavior than is culture. Researchers have consistently found that working families raise children with different values, attitudes, and behavior than do middle-class families throughout the world (Kagitcibasi, 1990; Lambert, Hamers, & Frasure-Smith, 1979). Working-class families tend to use punishment and negative reinforcement, such as "You're nothing and will never be any good at anything." Middle-class parents tend to emphasize positive reinforcement and activities designed to raise self-confidence and self-esteem.

Furthermore, culture is more important than gender. For example, in the general population, women experience more depression than men, supposedly because males act out their problems in a more active and vigorous manner through higher rates of alcoholism and antisocial behavior. However, among the Amish, there is no difference in the rates of depression between men and women, most probably because they perform very similar work and do not differentiate their social roles very clearly (Thase, Frank, & Kupfer, 1985).

EXERCISE 7.1   Social Class, Culture, and Gender

The instructor should ask students whether we can rank order these three factors—social class, culture, and gender—in terms of their importance in influencing values, attitudes, and behavior. That is, is social class most important, culture second, and gender third, as the material presented by the instructor suggests? Use think-pair-share, after which the instructor can make the following points:

- Importance varies by situation.

- Other studies may tend to contradict this rank ordering.

- There are statistical assumptions used in such a rank ordering that may not be valid.

EXERCISE 7.2   Culture Versus Social Class

The instructor can also show Figure 7.1 and ask: What kind of problems and behaviors would you expect to see in each of these four cells in terms of conflict and ease of interpersonal communication?

The instructor can make the point that there are frequently more difficulties communicating between social classes than between cultures. For example, many American tourists find that the French tend to be rude, but when two professionals from the United States and France meet, they tend to get along well. The instructor can also point out that culture becomes pivotal when key values are attacked, such as a war based significantly on the opposing religions of the two cultures. In this instance, differences in social class decrease in importance.

EXERCISE 7.3   Culture and Race

Given the information presented in Exercise 7.1, the instructor should ask, Is culture more important than race in explaining values, attitudes, and behavior? Use think-pair-share.

■ COMMENTS

The instructor can point out the following:

FIGURE 7.1.

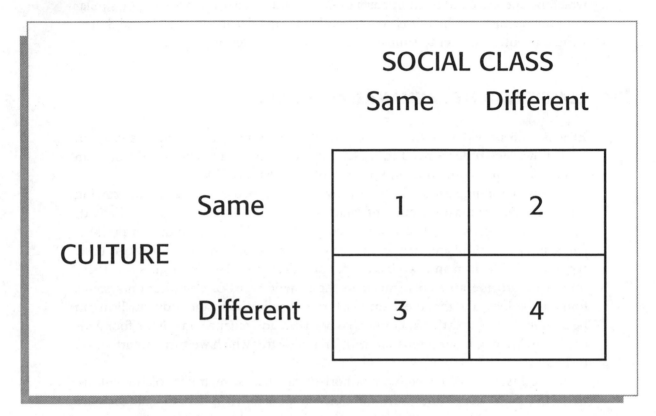

- Many experts feel that race is not a meaningful category, given the high rates of intermarriage and couplings. For example, a very large percentage of Americans are of mixed parentage.

- Social class is more important than race. It is the perception of opportunities that is crucial. Middle-class children, regardless of race, perceive the world as having more possibilities than do working-class children (Yando, Seitz, & Zigler, 1979).

EXERCISE 7.4   Culture and Institutions

The instructor can also ask, Is culture more important than key institutions, such as the legal system and the educational system? Use think-pair-share.

■ COMMENTS

Peng (in press) has reviewed the literature in this area and has concluded that institutions, particularly legal and economic frameworks, are more important for conducting business than are cultural similarities. For example, the manner in which business is conducted in parts of China and eastern Europe is more similar than the manner in which it is conducted between Taiwan and the United States. Peng attributes this fact to similar stages of economic development.

◼ CLASSIFICATION OF HUMAN RELATIONSHIPS

Exercise 7.5 provides synthesis of the material presented earlier in this chapter. First, however, students need to understand the basic points about individualism and collectivism as presented in the work of Triandis and Fiske.

As we have suggested, Hofstede provided the impetus for a large and growing body of important work, much of which emphasized different types of individualism and collectivism. The research completed by Harry Triandis (in press) is particularly insightful and helpful in management, because he identified two basic types of individualism and two basic types of collectivism. He also argues that these four types provide a schema similar to the generic types of classification systems found in biology, and that more specific forms of collectivism and individualism can be described after a particular culture has been categorized into one of the four general types. We begin our discussion with Triandis, after which we turn our attention to Fiske.

The first type of collectivism is horizontal, that is, members of the culture share the same values and even emotional responses, so much so that they are scarcely distinguishable from one another. Horizontal collectivism represents a high-context or process culture, and it is one in which there is little leeway given to members to deviate from norms and values. It is also a culture in which in-group members view out-groups in a frequently hostile fashion.

Under the second type, vertical collectivism, values are shared widely by in-group members, but there is an unequal distribution of power and authority. Typically, this form of collectivism emphasizes the "headman" style of leadership for both organizational and political leaders. The headman or national political leader has much greater authority, power, and prestige than others, but he is also responsible for ensuring that the cultural values are upheld and that members of the group are provided for. Most Americans have never experienced this style of leadership because it involves a reciprocal psychological relationship, that is, followers defer to the headman, who, in turn, is responsible for looking out for their welfare. For example, a bankrupt businessman will devote 3 years to ensuring that his former employees have jobs and are not homeless.

Individualism also is classified as horizontal and vertical. When a culture emphasizes horizontal individualism, its members make decisions by themselves without worrying about group considerations. However, such a culture also believes that equality is the norm that should be stressed rather than rankings based on power and prestige. Still, under vertical individualism, individuals do make decisions by themselves with minimal regard to group considerations, but there are prestige and power rankings in terms of authority, income, and so forth.

Independently, Alan Page Fiske (1994) arrived at these four basic types. Fiske goes far beyond Triandis and argues that there are four elementary forms of human relations. His work relies heavily on ethnographic data and integrating the theories and research of other researchers. Most importantly, Fiske basically employs the theory of numerical data as a metaphor underlying these four elementary forms.

In statistics, it is common to distinguish between the following types of data: nominal, ordinal, interval, and ratio. Nominal data basically means that classifications or groups are established, but there is no attempt to say that one category is greater or less than others. For example, a student could be a student in University X or University Y, but not both. With ordinal data, it is possible to say that some members of a group are greater or more important than other members, but the distance between members is not uniform, so that direct comparisons within the group are not possible. For example, John is more sociable than Mary, and Mary is more sociable than Peter, but it is not possible to say that John is twice as sociable as Peter. With interval data, there is a uniform distance between each point of the scale, but there is no true zero point; hence, you must compare individuals within a group in terms of each criterion. For example, John may be twice as sociable as Peter, but a new interval scale must be developed to compare them when criteria other than sociability are used. Finally, with ratio data there is a true zero point, which allows us either to transform every scale into a common unit of measurement or to aggregate all of the scales into one scale, for example, using money as reflective of a true zero point and paying individuals in terms of a composite score on several measures of performance.

Fiske argues that the first elementary form of human relations, Collective Sharing (CS), is based on nominal groupings: One is in either the in-group or the out-group, but not both. This corresponds to horizontal collectivism, and ethics is based on fulfilling the needs of all individuals within the group. Within the group, there is no such phenomenon as stealing because everything is shared, including food. However, out-group members are essentially treated as foreigners or barbarians and even nonhumans. This form is found in small and economically underdeveloped villages throughout the world.

The second elementary form, Authority Ranking (AR), is based on ordinal data and corresponds to vertical collectivism or the headman perspective on leadership. As suggested previously, subordinate individuals are very obsequious to those in power, and frequently, this is expressed in elaborate bows or gestures, such as holding hands in a praying position and then bowing much lower than the superior, who may merely nod in return. Such bowing is often seen in Asian nations, such as Japan and Thailand, and it is in marked contrast to the Western handshake, which connotes only a greeting signifying equality on the part of those engaging in it. In an AR culture, ethics is based on status rather than need, and those at the higher rank receive proportionately more of the goods and rewards, even though they are expected to fulfill more responsibilities than those lower in status and power.

Horizontal individualism is characteristic of the third elementary form, Equality Matching (EM). Individual decision making is respected and encouraged, even at the group's expense, or at least of some of its members. However, members of such a cultural group believe that some individuals will be superior to others on one measure but not another, because the measurement must be taken each time. In such national cultures, everyone is assumed to be equal, and ethical norms are based on this assumption. At the same time, it is assumed that everyone will make an equitable or equal contribution to the group, although the timing is not specified. The Scandinavian nations have constructed a social and cultural system in which EM is practiced, because they have very high but regressive tax rates and, at the same time, the highest charitable contributions on a per capita basis of all developed nations.

Finally, there is Market Pricing (MP), which emphasizes a true zero point: money. Everything can be expressed in terms of money, and so it is now possible to rank individuals on several criteria and to compare their values directly across these criteria. Some criteria will be more important than others and will be so weighted, but it is now possible to come to a final, aggregated score for each individual. MP corresponds to vertical individualism, and it is the basis for performance evaluation in many nations, including the United States. In such a culture, a person's worth is assessed vis-à-vis that of others, and this worth can change dramatically over time.

EXERCISE 7.5 — The Four Basic Types of Human Relations

Fiske provides some insightful examples of the manner in which these four elementary forms are played out in actual decisions. He asks the reader to consider the purchase of an expensive fire truck by a small town of 10,000. At this point, the instructor should ask,

- Who should pay for the fire truck? Some residents are so poor that they do not even pay taxes supporting such activities.

- In the four situations using different forms of human relations, whose homes should be protected?

The instructor can use think-pair-share, after which he or she can point out the following:

- Under CS, everyone's home is protected, even if he or she did not help to pay for the new truck.

- Under AR, everyone is protected, but the more important people receive additional protection. For example, the fire truck goes by their homes four times more frequently.

- Under EM, everyone is protected, because it is assumed that everyone is contributing equally or will contribute more when able to do so.

- Under MP, only those paying taxes are protected. In fact, it is not unusual in the United States for a home to burn down because its owners did not pay taxes and/or the home is outside of a nearby jurisdiction that does have a fire truck readily available.

As this discussion indicates, the use of a numerical measurement metaphor greatly enhances our understanding. The instructor can probe by asking the following questions:

- How effective would "pay for performance" be in each of these four cultural systems?

- When a nation such as Indonesia is ruled by one person for decades, which cultural form of human relations is being used?

- How can this framework be used to analyze organizational and cultural change?

EXERCISE 7.6 An Ethical Dilemma

Assume you are a businessman who has traveled to an Asian country with the intent of selling your company's product. Because you have cross-cultural training, you understand that relationship building is a key part of the process. Things appear to be going well; you and three of your counterparts have been enjoying one another's company over several drinks together at a local nightspot. Your first negotiating session is scheduled for the next morning.

At the end of the evening, as people are preparing to leave, two of the men exit briefly and return with a beautiful young woman. They tell you that she is a gift from them to show their appreciation of you. You are a happily married man with several children at home. What do you do? You do not want to offend them, but you have grave ethical concerns with this activity. You have been warned that this is a standard business practice in some parts of the world.

The instructor can use the Fiske framework (Exercise 7.5) to focus the discussion. He or she can then point out that refusing such a gift will not influence the business relationship negatively. However, the refusal should be polite so as to save face, for example, "I am too tired and just want to be alone."

EXERCISE 7.7 Preparing for an International Assignment

The instructor can point out that international assignments of both short and long duration are very common. Use think-pair-share and ask how class members would prepare for an international assignment that will last at least 1 year.

The instructor can then go over the following means of preparation:

- Read everything you can find about the country and the culture
- Contact the embassy
- Look at maps
- Understand the means of exchange
- Gain an expectation of the housing
- Gain at least a basic knowledge of the language
- Talk to native and non-native residents
- Visit tourist agencies
- Learn "do's and don'ts" from travel books
- Take a course on the country at a local university

The instructor can also indicate that the following activities can help to integrate a person into a culture:

- Go to church or other house of worship and meet people
- Read the local newspaper daily
- Identify and join social groups
- Observe where people congregate
- Follow the dress code—do not stand out too much
- Invite people to lunch
- Do not reject invitations
- Stay near or with natives
- Show interest in the culture and history
- Do not be judgmental
- Learn how to get around the city
- Adopt the time schedule of the country
- Try to form deeper relationships
- Listen to local radio and television
- Avoid tourist spots
- Study art and architecture
- Be patient

EXERCISE 7.8   Life Lesson

This exercise is based on information provided in "Life Lesson" (1997).

Hong Xiaohui is a Chinese worker who, like millions of others, migrated from the poorer central region to the Chinese coastal region seeking a better life. Initially, she found a factory job doing menial labor but became disenchanted with the work and living conditions. She then returned home to start her own business before once again traveling to the coastal region on a second attempt.

Hong came to realize that a better financial life is available in the more industrial coastal towns, but there are drawbacks. For her, such drawbacks included the promise of promotion if she agreed to become the boss's girlfriend. It seemed that everything was a trade-off, including the biggest decision of whether to trade her ideals for financial freedom.

Quite often, factories require that workers put in 12 or more hours of performing routine and tedious work. They also may require that a worker live in factory dorms, which have many restrictions as well as poor conditions. All told, although she was happy to be away from home and on her own, it was a very strict environment, and no one looked out for her.

Hong eventually tired of the conditions and once again left her factory job and returned home. With her savings and new skills in business, she opened a restaurant that has been quite successful. But being back home meant she had to respect parents in all matters, including breaking up with a boyfriend who did not gain their approval.

The instructor can use think-pair-share and ask students to apply the Fiske framework to this situation (Exercise 7.5). He or she can also ask the students to apply the cultural metaphor of the Chinese Family Altar to this situation (see Gannon & Associates, 2001).

CHAPTER 8

Cross-Cultural Negotiations

As businesspeople increasingly interact with those of other national and ethnic cultures, they need to understand the process of negotiation. This chapter is a brief introduction to this topic, with special attention devoted to cross-cultural issues.

EXERCISE 8.1a Rug Negotiations: Part 1

The instructor should divide the class into dyads. Give one member of each dyad Figure 8.1 and the other member Figure 8.2. Negotiations should then take place for 15 minutes, at the end of which the instructor should write on the board the final offers made by each seller and each buyer and the difference in these offers (three columns). The instructor should then ask for reactions to the exercise. Typically, many of these reactions are spirited and/or negative, such as "The buyer made such an insulting offer that I would never sell to him."

The instructor should then introduce the two major types of bargaining—distributive and integrative. Distributive bargaining assumes that there is a fixed number of points over which the buyer and seller are bargaining. Integrative bargaining makes no such assumption. Rather, the negotiators look for creative ways for satisfying both buyer and seller.

Then, the instructor should introduce the five styles of bargaining (see Figure 8.3). He or she should point out that one of these styles is not negotiating (withdrawal), because the individual does not wish to satisfy the party. Only the style in which both parties are trying to satisfy each other and themselves simultaneously represents integrative bargaining. The other three styles are distributive by definition.

The instructor should also go over Ronald Burke's classic study of these five styles among managers and supervisors. He asked a few hundred of them to give examples when they resolved a problem effectively, and then to give examples when they resolved a problem ineffectively (Burke, 1979). When problems were resolved effectively, the problem-solving or integrative style was employed by 58.5% of the respondents, the forcing style by 24.5%, and the compromise style by 11.3%; the other examples could not be classified (5.7%). When problems were resolved ineffectively, the overwhelming majority (79.2%) employed the forcing style and 0.0% the problem-solving style. These results suggest that the problem-solving or integrative style is much more effective than the other styles, and only occasionally are any of the other styles effective. This includes the forcing style, which is common among many negotiators.

EXERCISE 8.1b — Rug Negotiations: Part 2

Returning to the rug negotiation, the instructor can usually highlight the following points:

- Most of the dyads negotiated distributively and did not try to satisfy both parties.

- Integrative solutions tend to be more complex and creative, for example, the buyer will leave a deposit of 500 units and send additional money to the seller when he returns home, and the seller will make such concessions as providing an additional small rug.

- When one party feels that the other party is not genuinely negotiating, he or she will tend to become angry and stop bargaining.

- The distributive approach tends to result in less satisfaction and closure of the deal than does the integrative or problem-solving approach.

- The value that one party attaches to the rug may be different from the value that the other party attaches to it. One should avoid this problem by seeking information.

EXERCISE 8.1c — Rug Negotiations: Part 3

The instructor may then want to show the AMA video featuring Ken Thomas as he explains these five styles in detail (see Chapter 11). He may also want to review the Fisher, Ury, and Patton book *Getting to Yes* (1991). They compare a soft bargainer (someone so concerned about satisfying the other party that he or she fails to satisfy or consider his or her own interests) to a hard bargainer (someone very concerned

FIGURE 8.1. The Seller

You are the owner of a store in a country of your choice (one with which you are familiar). You sell rugs, pillowcases, and other articles of housewares. You notice on this particular day that a foreign visitor is interested in a particular rug.

There are many other stores that sell similar rugs for about 700 units. This particular rug seems to be of much better quality and is a very special shade of green. This particular rug costs you 750 units. You normally sell this rug for 1,000 to 1,200 units.

This store is your sole source of income.

There are many possibilities besides just price that you can use to make a deal. *Feel free to use your creativity and imagination.*

FIGURE 8.2. The Buyer

You are visiting a foreign country and would like to buy a rug as a present for your spouse.

You are currently in a store that sells rugs, pillowcases, and other articles of housewares, and you have found a very nice rug that would look great in the living room. You have seen similar rugs in this area of the country. Friends of yours tell you that you can buy rugs here for 600 units. This particular rug seems to be of much better quality and is a very special shade of green that your spouse would really like and that you have not seen before. You have fallen in love with it.

You have only 1,000 units left in your wallet, and this is to last the rest of your journey. You leave the day after tomorrow for home.

FIGURE 8.3. Strategies and Methods for Resolving Conflict

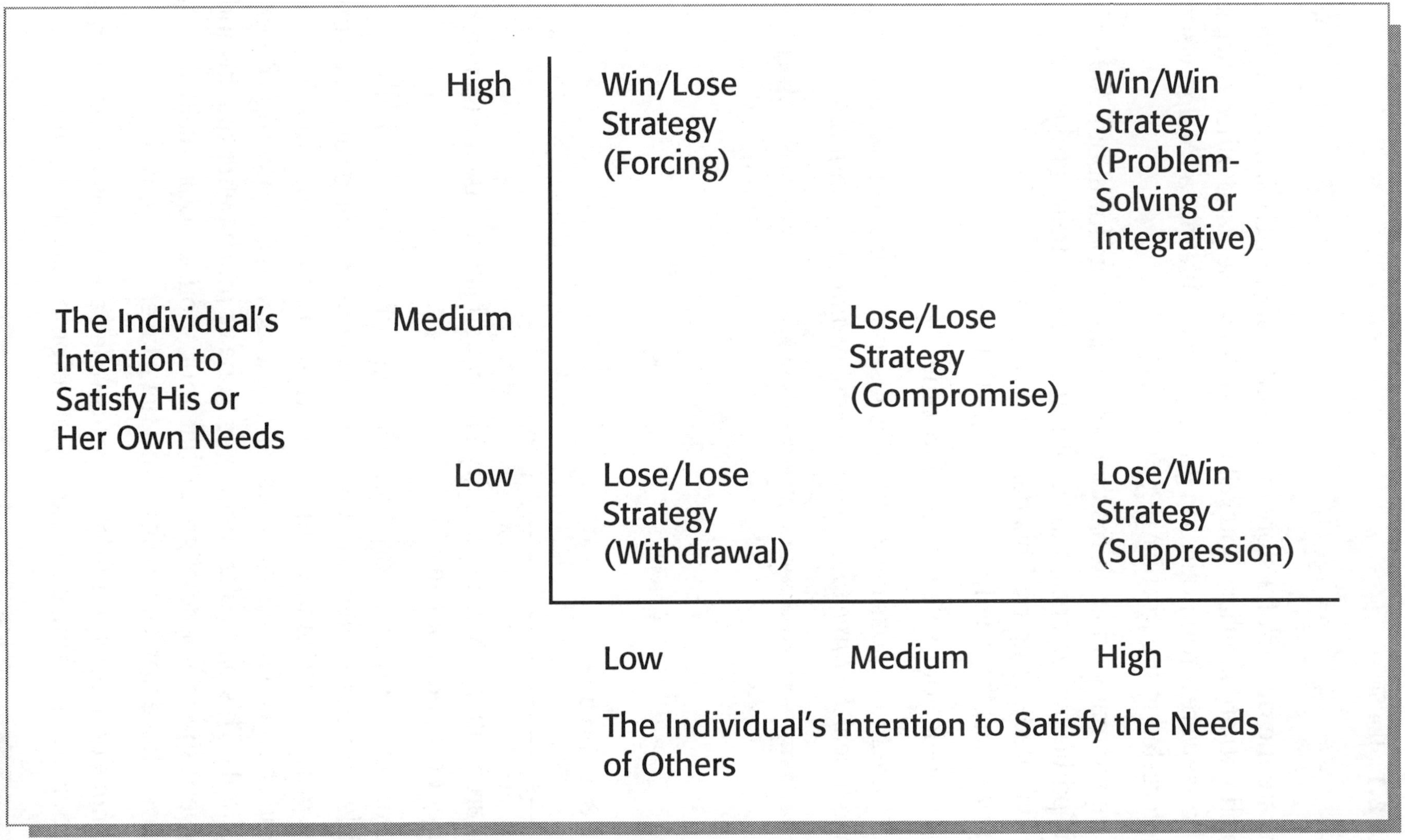

The figure is a grid plotting "The Individual's Intention to Satisfy His or Her Own Needs" (vertical axis: High, Medium, Low) against "The Individual's Intention to Satisfy the Needs of Others" (horizontal axis: Low, Medium, High):

- High / Low: Win/Lose Strategy (Forcing)
- High / High: Win/Win Strategy (Problem-Solving or Integrative)
- Medium / Medium: Lose/Lose Strategy (Compromise)
- Low / Low: Lose/Lose Strategy (Withdrawal)
- Low / High: Lose/Win Strategy (Suppression)

about satisfying himself or herself and has no interest in satisfying the other party). The instructor may want to ask, When a tough bargainer and a soft bargainer negotiate, who wins? Clearly, the hard bargainer.

The Fisher, Ury, and Patton integrative model consists of four parts:

- Separate the *people* from the problem

- Focus on *interests* of both parties, not their positions

- Invent *options* or complex solutions for mutual gains

- Use objective *criteria,* and, if possible, establish them before the bargaining begins

Fisher et al. recommend that the negotiator has in mind his or her best alternative to a negotiated agreement, or BATNA. That is, at what point is the negotiator willing to walk away from the negotiation because he or she will not receive at least minimal satisfaction?

Herb Cohen (1982) has developed a similar model, but his book is filled with many practical examples, some of which provoke ethical discussions. In general, this book espouses the integrative approach, but it does indicate that sometimes, a person will face a Soviet-style negotiator who is an extreme version of the hard bargainer, in which case more extreme measures need to be taken. Cohen's model includes three factors:

- *Information.* The more information a negotiator has, the better off he or she is.

- *Time.* Do not let the other side know when you must quit negotiating, because that gives them more power and more information.

- *Power.* To Cohen, power is simply the ability to get things done; thus, it is ethically neutral. The more information the negotiator has, and the more he or she is able to control the pace and timing of the negotiation, the more powerful he or she is.

EXERCISE 8.2   Key Rules of Negotiating

There are several key rules for negotiating. Before identifying them, the instructor can ask class members to identify their key rules for negotiating, after which he or she can present the following:

- Listen more than you talk, as listening helps to provide information and power.

- In general, do not become emotional. Use an emotional outburst only when you are employing it as a negotiating tactic, for example, walking out of the room when you know the other side will beg you to come back.

- In general, do not agree to a settlement immediately. Take a break for a few minutes, or at least think about the agreement silently for at least a minute before agreeing. Having a trip wire, such as saying that you need to consult with your spouse before accepting a job offer, leaves you room for thought and maneuver.

- Many people assume that the other side will not accept a high offer, and so they never make it. Be reasonable, but make initial high offers, or initial high counter-offers if an offer has already been made.

- If you face a hard or difficult bargainer, openly bring up this issue.

- Be prepared, and take notes, because you tend to forget what has been said throughout the negotiations.

- Periodically summarize, identifying the key points of agreement and the key points requiring additional negotiation.

- If the negotiation proves difficult, focus on a settlement range and not a specific point within it, and indicate that you are willing to bargain within this range as long as the other party is agreeable to the concept of mutually satisfying and creative solutions.

- When bargaining cross-culturally, be sensitive to cross-cultural issues, such as the need to save face.

- Remember that all negotiations go through stages, and that in the early stages, the focus should be more on processes than outcomes, especially when the other side comes from a high-context culture.

- Do not close a deal unless you are satisfied both logically and emotionally.

- Try to convince the other side that you are at your bottom line and may need to invoke your BATNA.

- Remember that trust is key to a negotiation, even if it involves a one-time inter-action. Try to establish a psychological relationship.

- Use simple language to avoid misunderstandings.

The instructor can also use Figure 8.4 at this point.

Weiss (1994) has provided some additional suggestions for negotiating cross-culturally. If you have low familiarity with the counterpart's culture, employ an agent or advisor, involve a mediator, induce the counterpart to follow your script, or adapt to the counterpart's script. If you have only moderate familiarity with the counterpart's culture, try to coordinate the adjustment of both parties and embrace the counterpart's script. If you have high familiarity with the counterpart's culture, improvise an approach or create a "symphony" or creative solution that is very appealing to both sides.

EXERCISE 8.3   Metaphors for Negotiations

Michele Gelfand of the Psychology Department at the University of Maryland at College Park created this exercise. She provides the instructions for identifying your own metaphor for negotiations (see Figure 8.5).

FIGURE 8.4.

Types of bargaining

- Distributive: assumes only a fixed number of points or a mixed pie

- Integrative: assumes that the fixed nature of the bargaining process can be changed through meeting the needs of both parties

Conditions for the success of integrative bargaining

- Creative options

- Complex proposals

- Specifying criteria up front

- Creating trust

- Realistic bargaining

- Understanding one another

- Listening

- Controlling emotions

This is a very effective exercise. Many people bring to the surface their fear of negotiating by using such metaphors as being a crab at the beach and being afraid of the natural elements, a maze from which it is difficult to extricate oneself, and so on. As an alternative to the written exercise, the instructor can use think-pair-share, asking class members to identify their metaphors and to have discussions in pairs, after which there is a class discussion. Some popular metaphors are poker, chess, dancing, fist fight in the schoolyard, tennis match, volleyball, and football.

EXERCISE 8.4   Collecting No's Cross-Culturally

Jeffrey Ford (in Lewicki, Saunders, & Minton, 1999) has developed a very effective exercise for the timid or less-assured negotiator. Many people fail at negotiations because they believe they know what the other side wants and will do. Moreover, many—perhaps most—people tend to assume that both sides will place the same value on the object under consideration, and they do not like to confront issues and people directly. But frequently, such assumptions are unwarranted. To demonstrate graphically the weaknesses of such assumptions, this exercise stipulates that a student or trainee go out and specifically ask ten individuals to do something that is doable but not very reasonable. For example, one manager asked fellow managers to give her $20 that she did not plan to repay! Six of the ten individuals actually gave her the $20 rather than saying "No" to the request. Needless to say, students and trainees are eager to reflect upon and talk about their experiences, as such experiences are at great variance with their original mindsets.

Ford has established the following rules:

- Requests must be legal
- You cannot tell people why you are making the request
- The request must involve something that the person can really do, even if it seems unreasonable
- Each request must be different
- A minimum of ten different people must be asked

■ COMMENTS

This is a powerful exercise, and people are frequently very surprised at the outcomes. For example, one student asked people at work for $20 but indicated that she was not planning to pay them back. Even so, most gave the $20!

For the cross-cultural focus, the instructor can ask the student to ask five people from his or her same cultural group and five other people. The instructor can also ask that students write up the results or be prepared to engage in a class discussion. No matter the approach, students like this exercise.

FIGURE 8.5. Metaphor and Negotiation Exercise

Please include this information in your two journal entries, in addition to the information specified in the syllabus.

We are interested in finding out about the contexts to which people compare their negotiation experiences. In order to describe their negotiation experiences, people often compare them to other domains of their lives. This mapping of one domain onto another is known as a *metaphor.* People often use metaphors in their daily lives, sometimes without even knowing that they are doing so. For instance, you could describe learning to ski as being like a first date because of your nervousness and clumsiness. Or, you may think that the brain processes information like a computer.

Please think about negotiations in which you have participated. What kinds of metaphors would you use to describe these experiences? That is, we would like you to answer the question "Negotiation is like _____," and consider *why* the two domains are related. When responding, please consider the goals, rules, and activities that you think are involved in negotiation, and then think of a domain in which such goals, rules, and activities are also operating. Feel free to come up with more than one metaphor if you wish.

EXERCISE 8.5   **Alpha and Beta Styles**

Lewicki et al. (1999) have developed an excellent bargaining simulation that involves one party using the high-context, process approach while the other party employs the low-context, outcome-focused approach. More than one individual can be a member of each negotiating group. Please consult this book and its accompanying Instructor's Manual for details.

AMERICAN, JAPANESE, AND GERMAN STYLES OF NEGOTIATING

A study reported in the *Wall Street Journal* ("Side by Side," 1994) noted that in 1993, IBM established a joint venture research team to develop a revolutionary new chip design for the next century. The other companies in the group were Siemens AG of Germany and Toshiba Corporation of Japan. Engineers from all three companies were set up in Long Island at one of IBM's research affiliates. The project was expected to last several years.

People who initially were worried that the more than 100 scientists from the three countries would have difficulties working together proved to be correct. Problems began almost immediately. Individuals wanted to associate only with fellow country members, thus jeopardizing the project's success. An observer noted that the Japanese disliked the office setup, which consisted of many small offices and few open spaces, and they had difficulty conversing in English. The Germans covered the glass walls of their offices to maintain privacy, thus offending both the Japanese and Americans. The Japanese liked to go out drinking after work, during which time they tended to develop strong group norms. The Americans, however, preferred to go home to their families. Furthermore, the Americans complained that the Germans planned too much and that the Japanese would not make decisions.

Catherine Tinsley (1998) writes that each of the three cultures has an inherent and culturally based method for resolving conflict. She outlines these three methods as follows.

- *The Status Model:* Preferred by the Japanese, this model assumes that when there is conflict, one should defer to status power within the group. Therefore, those with the highest status will have the power to create and enforce resolutions for the group, and they will be accepted and respected by all (see Exercise 7.5).

- *Applying Regulations:* This method is preferred by the Germans, and it emphasizes referring back to preexisting independent regulations, rules, and policies to shape the resolution of a conflict.

- *Integrating Interests:* The Americans prefer this negotiation style of conflict resolution. It involves incorporating the concerns of all parties in an attempt to create an outcome most worthwhile to the entire group.

EXERCISE 8.6

American, Japanese, and German Styles of Negotiating

Have students work in small groups to apply Tinsley's methods to the IBM case. How should the group solve its problems to ensure the success of the project?

■ COMMENTS

The *Wall Street Journal* article continues to discuss some solutions that IBM used, including a plan to stress cooperative efforts through joint training among the three companies. This method would make each group more aware of the management and working styles in the other two countries. Also, they instituted more work teams consisting of culturally mixed groups, and they encouraged more socialization outside of the work environment. The buddy system was also used to assign each foreign worker a local buddy to help show him or her the ropes. The idea was to create an environment where creativity was enhanced rather than stifled. It is believed that this is extremely important in a development environment, where a creative breakthrough is as likely to occur in the lunchroom as in the laboratory. IBM hoped that these changes would further that cause.

CHAPTER 9

A Metaphor in Depth: The German Symphony

In this chapter, there is an extended treatment of the manner in which the instructor can teach about a specific cultural metaphor, the German Symphony. The treatment is based on the chapter about the German Symphony in Gannon and Associates (2001).

■ CHAPTER OVERVIEW

1. Narrative Summary

   The metaphor used for Germany is the symphony orchestra. German culture is represented by the symphony's staying power, its harmonization of individuals and their talents into an intricate and beautiful work of art, and its well-developed organization and complex set of rules.

2. Chapter Performance Objectives

   At the conclusion of this chapter, students should be able to

   a. describe Germany's cultural characteristics and dimensions in terms of the symphony metaphor

   b. apply their understanding of German values embodied in the symphony to improve professional and personal relationships with members of the German culture

111

◤ DISCUSSION OF THE CULTURE

1. Description of the Metaphor

   Key Points to Cover

   a. The symphonic music art form is centuries old. It was developed in the 16th century in Germany using the Italian operatic overture as a starting point and expanding it to several movements, typically three.

   b. Symphony music is written to blend sections of a large number of different types of instruments into one harmonious, beautiful musical sound.

   c. Individual musicians must be highly talented and well trained, yet willing to perform most of the time as part of a large group rather than as soloists.

   d. Successful symphony performances require a skilled leader or conductor to coordinate all of the individual musicians.

   e. Precision and synchronicity are critical to achieving a flawless performance.

   f. The symphony is an idealized, elaborate, and traditional form of music that requires great musical and economic resources and much practice to perfect.

   Question for Discussion

   a. How well does a symphony work as a metaphor for German culture?

2. The Country's History and Current Economic and Political Situation

   Key Points to Cover

   a. Continually shifting borders over the course of history and the Germans' desire for unity, symbolized by the concept of a German nation, the Fatherland, is reflected in the unified musical presentation of numerous musicians in the symphony.

   b. The Germans' desire for unity also led to their acceptance of the sacrifices required to unify East and West Germany as well as their support of a unified European Union.

   c. The Germans' sense of history is reflected in their appreciation of the centuries-old symphony tradition.

   d. The Germans' idealized view of their country as wealthy, successful, and culturally advanced is reflected in the symphony's grandeur and elegance.

   e. The Germans' pride in their county's accomplishments in science and the arts is reflected in their identification with many of the finest symphonic composers as fellow countrymen.

   Questions for Discussion

   a. How do Germans tend to deal with their country's responsibility for the Holocaust and WWII? How do these events affect their desire to perceive themselves as well-schooled, finely cultured people?

   b. How have Germany's numerous contributions in the sciences and the arts affected German culture? Consider inventions, particularly the printing press and its impact on communication; scientific theories; and the birth of Protestantism. Also consider indirect effects, such as the response of other countries to these contributions and changes in Germany's status among other nations as a result of these contributions.

3. Cultural Dimensions

Key Points to Cover

a. Cultural characteristics

(1) Perception of the individual: Like most Christians, Germans tend to believe that individuals have tremendous potential—they are capable of producing music that approaches perfection; however, they also tend to believe that humans are extremely fallible and must constantly strive to avoid failure.

(2) Perceptions of the world: Germany has an intriguing perception of the world based on the symphony metaphor. The role of individuals is to perform to the best of their ability as a small part of the harmony that is the symphony; yet Germans get the most pleasure out of the natural beauty of music, flowers, and the beach if they can experience them in a very ordered, controlled fashion, all of which suggests a dominant orientation.

(3) Personal relationships: Germany is more collectivistic than the United States, but less collectivistic than most Asian societies, as shown by the importance and the submission of the individual musician in the symphony.

(4) Activity: With their careful composition of lengthy musical pieces and their disciplined practice of the music, the symphony's musicians demonstrate that Germans very much feel that they can control the results of their actions to improve their quality of life.

(5) Time
   (a) Like symphony music that can be carefully arranged linearly on the musical score so that each musician stays in sync with the entire orchestra as the piece progresses, Germans conduct life according to a linear perception of time, with all important activities scheduled so that they can be completed efficiently and on time.
   (b) Germans have a fairly balanced past-present-future time orientation, with a little greater emphasis on the present and the future; although Germans appreciate the tradition of the symphony, they are always working to improve future performances, and as a performance, the musical art of the symphony is always experienced very much in the present by the audience.

(6) Space
   (a) As in the orchestra, where every musician has a specific role (e.g., first-chair violin), German space is also divided into very specific functional areas that offer privacy and allow concentration on the task at hand.

(b) Germans extend the functionality of space to personal space as well: They do not welcome unplanned visits to their homes, intrusions upon their private leisure time, or encroachment upon the physical and aural space they occupy.

b. Cultural dimensions of work behavior (Hofstede, 1980)

(1) Power distance: Germany scores below the median, a little lower than the United States.

(a) Although the conductor is an authority figure, he gets the authority by earning the respect of the musicians, who choose to follow only if the conductor is competent and talented; therefore, consensus is the primary mode of decision making.

(b) The German educational system provides a good education for every German child in keeping with German respect for the individual and equality; however, just as professional musicians generally master one particular musical instrument, so, too, a German child is generally assigned to a school that will educate him or her in a particular vocation according to his or her aptitude, which is determined by standardized tests.

(2) Uncertainty avoidance: Germany scores above the median, somewhat higher than the United States.

(a) Conformity is valued, as is the musicians' submission to the direction of the orchestra conductor.

(b) Germany has many rules, as does the art of symphonic music: Public signs describing acceptable or forbidden behaviors are everywhere.

(c) The German educational apprenticeship systems are well-ordered to ensure that students are properly trained and prepared for productive jobs in the real world after they graduate, just as rehearsals are held to ensure that a symphonic orchestra is prepared to meet the expectations of its audience.

(d) Germans believe strongly that they know what is right and what is wrong, similar to their belief that Germans know best how to compose, play, and conduct symphonic music.

(e) Timing is critical to the unified harmonies of the symphony; likewise, schedules are strictly followed in business to ensure that meetings take place and important business gets done.

(f) The Germans' love for tradition tends to make them more comfortable with old friends and familiar activities and less interested in trying new things, meeting new people, or taking risks.

(3) Individualism: Germany scores fairly high, about halfway between the median and the United States' score in Hofstede's (1980) study.

(a) The individual is encouraged to develop personal talent to the fullest and is recognized for expertise and abilities, whether in business or in the orchestra.

(b) Individual talents are contributed to the achievement of a common goal, just like symphony instruments are played in harmony to create one sound.

(c) Like symphony musicians who do not have much choice about the music they will perform, German children are directed to an education and a career that their parents and teachers feel is suited for them.

(d) The Germans' belief that they know what is right and what is wrong leads to enthusiastic participation in politics and a variety of interest groups; however, although a minority of Germans feel that their certainty about their beliefs entitles them to infringe upon the political rights of others, most Germans are the opposite and are very tolerant of other points of view.

(4) Masculinity: Germans score above the median, about the same as the United States. Germans' interest in improving themselves and achieving goals such as a beautiful symphonic performance is evidence of their slightly masculine orientation.

Questions for Discussion

a. How should business visitors to Germany expect to be received if they arrive at the office of the professional they have come to see during working hours? What should visitors expect if they are being picked up at the airport after working hours by the same person?

b. What would be a good expression of gratitude for a German host's or hostess's hospitality?

c. Germany's education system has been very successful in producing a highly skilled, productive workforce. Is there a downside to the German educational system? If so, what changes should be made, and how could those changes be implemented so that they would be accepted into German culture?

d. If an American expatriate's children are accustomed to playing sports at home, how might they need to adjust their attitudes or approach to sports to enjoy playing them in Germany?

e. If a German feels that here is a better way to get a job done than the way you are following, what action might you expect him or her to take?

4. Religious Values

Key Points to Cover

a. Christianity's emphasis on Christ's death and resurrection may contribute to a German superstition that great leaders will return to Germany's times of need, like a retired conductor who comes back to full-time work.

b. Christianity teaches that each individual has duties in both public and private life and that the Bible clarifies these duties; similarly, a successful symphony performance requires that each member of the orchestra follow the score and the conductor's direction.

    c. Christianity is also an egalitarian religion whose leaders were chosen from the common people based upon their performance as followers of Christ, much as the conductor becomes a leader after first becoming a proficient musician.

    d. In keeping with their reverence for tradition, the majority of Germans still observe all of the major Christian holidays. Approximately half the German population is Catholic, and the other half is Protestant.

Questions for Discussion

    a. How important are the Germans' religious values in determining their behavior or influencing their decisions?

    b. To what extent do the Germans' religious values affect their everyday routines?

5. Personal Lives and Relationships

Key Points to Cover

    a. Many Germans play musical instruments as a serious hobby to which they devote time and energy because music is a source of deep enrichment for them.

    b. Like symphonic music, Germans' lives are well planned and orchestrated so that they make effective, efficient use of family, social, and work time, which are rarely combined.

    c. Tradition and formality are revered in the symphony as well as in German social customs, such as the use of surnames and formal personal pronouns for all but the closest friends, courteous manners, and the slow development of friendships.

    d. Germans expect a high degree of beauty, expertise, and quality from a symphony's musicians and, likewise, their possessions.

    e. The German appreciation for beauty extends from music to flowers, but beauty is controlled formally in both symphonies and German flower gardens.

    f. Germans enjoy participating in active leisure pursuits such as traditional festivals, hiking, and sports in groups, but, in keeping with their functionalized view of the world, they do not enjoy getting personal with casual acquaintances; they keep personal relationships to a select few friends and family members.

Questions for Discussion

    a. How effective are overtime pay and promises of getting ahead in motivating the average German worker to work overtime? What other incentives might be worth trying?

    b. Does the typical German worker expect his or her manager to be concerned about any aspects of his or her personal life? How about those aspects that might specifically affect his or her work?

    c. Do German workers tend to socialize with one another outside of work?

    d. Is there a causal relationship between Germans' formality and their development of only a few very close personal friendships or vice versa? If so, which seems to be the cause, and which is the effect?

6. Professional Lives and Working Relationships (motivation, leadership decision making, planning accomplishment, communication style, business strengths, and business weaknesses)

Key Points to Cover

    a. Successful individual performance is allowed in symphonic solos and in business, but aggressive ambition and unwillingness to work as part of a group ruins the harmony and is discouraged in both.

    b. Successful German leaders are typically visionaries who, like the conductor of an orchestra, have a vision of how the future can be improved; can engender enthusiasm for this vision among their followers; and can organize, delegate, and manage work effectively among the individuals in the group. But, with the notable exception of Hitler, they are not charismatic.

    c. Each musician in an orchestra is responsible for learning and knowing his or her part perfectly; likewise, each member of a German business organization is responsible for and has a great deal of authority with respect to his or her own job function.

    d. The conductor must have the consensus of dozens of musicians to achieve a harmonious symphonic sound, and the ideal German business decision is also made and implemented through consensus. Although it is laborious to reach a decision, once it is reached, it is implemented quickly, and commitments are almost always met. This participatory approach to management and decision making has resulted in good labor relations.

    e. Germans give their leisure time as much priority as their work time; they guard their time for both with equal jealousy.

Questions for Discussion

    a. The book cites Hitler as a German leader who does *not* fit the leadership ideal symbolized by the conductor of an orchestra. Do you agree or disagree?

    b. How quickly should an American manager expect to receive a decision from a German counterpart? Does it depend upon whether the decision is one that the German manager will make alone, or one that involves a number of his or her co-workers?

    c. Once a decision is made, will implementation go quickly? Will it go smoothly? How reliable are Germans in keeping their commitments?

    d. Are German workers generally on time? What kind of absenteeism should an American manager expect from German workers?

    e. What type of management style will work well for an American manager assigned to a position in Germany? Have the students try to answer the question using management and conflict management models (see Chapter 8).

■ ACTIVITIES AND EXERCISES

The following activities can be used in any combination to help reinforce the symphony metaphor for German culture with visual, hands-on, and/or multi-sensory learning experiences.

1. Role Playing

   Have students act out ordinary business situations, such as a group project meeting, a job interview, or a performance review. Have at least one student in each group role-play a native for 5 to 10 minutes while others act the way they normally would given the situation. If possible, have each student try playing the German for a short time. At the end of the allotted time, debrief the entire class together, and ask students to comment on those aspects of their assumed role that were the most difficult for them to adjust to. Students will role-play more effectively if the activity takes place after an in-depth discussion of the metaphor (see Exercise 8.6).

2. Listen to a Symphony

   Use a video or audio recording of a symphony orchestra playing a piece by a German composer, or arrange a field trip to see a performance live. Be sure to choose a performance with a full orchestra rather than a smaller ensemble so that students can appreciate the complexity of the music and its arrangement. Ask the students to discuss the entire experience and relate its sound, mood, presentation, and components to the discussion of German culture. Listening to the symphony before the metaphor discussion can greatly enhance the students' use of the metaphor elements in the discussion, although the activity is also beneficial if used to reinforce the discussion afterwards. This activity also can be enhanced if a member of the music faculty can be recruited to provide a brief discourse on the musical components of the symphony.

3. Case Analysis

   Choose a case that illustrates a cross-cultural problem involving a German worker or organization. Ask the students to complete a case analysis, either as part of their homework assignment or in class in groups. They should use the metaphor to support their conclusions about the contribution of German cultural traits to the problem. Students' recommendations should be supported with a German's basic values; they should show that their recommended strategy fits into the value system by referring back to the symphony metaphor. The case should be completed after reading the chapter or after the class discussion.

4. Guest Speaker

   Have a native German, preferably someone involved in management who has had experience in cross-cultural business settings, come and relate their experience to the class. If possible, it would be particularly interesting to have a native German guest speaker in conjunction with either the role-playing exercise or the case analysis so that he or she could provide accurate critiques of the students' understanding of the German culture.

If it is not possible to arrange for a native German speaker, perhaps an international manager with a great deal of business experience in Germany could be scheduled. This type of speaker may not offer the same depth of insight into the German culture as a native could, but he or she will have a lot of experiences to talk about from the point of view of the foreign manager trying to learn the ropes.

◼ CHAPTER PERFORMANCE REVIEW

1. Students' Review of Their Previous and Current Perceptions of the Culture

   Questions for Discussion

   a. How accurate were the students' preconceptions of the German culture?

   b. Were there major aspects of the German culture of which the students had been unaware before reading the metaphor chapter?

2. Review the Chapter Performance Objectives

   The following questions will help the instructor evaluate student contribution to class discussion to determine whether or not the chapter objectives have been met.

   a. Were students able to use the symphony metaphor fluently in describing Germany's cultural characteristics and dimensions?

   b. Were students able to readily apply their understanding of German values embodied in the symphony to either activities simulating interactions with Germans or hypothetical business situations involving German colleagues?

A Metaphor in Depth: The Japanese Garden

Chapter 10 follows the same format as Chapter 9. The focus is on an extended treatment of one cultural metaphor, the Japanese garden.

◤ CHAPTER OVERVIEW

1. Narrative Summary

    The metaphor used to describe Japan is the wet garden. The fluidity yet essentially unchanging nature of the water in the pond's garden illustrates how the Japanese perceive their culture's change over time. Water's composition of tiny, individual droplets that have power only when combined with others parallels the Japanese view of the individual. The transient disturbance of a rock thrown into the pond demonstrates the Japanese understanding of the momentary impact but essential separateness of foreign ideas and cultures. And the beauty, tranquillity, and oneness of the garden with nature are illustrative of the Japanese values of harmony and aesthetics.

2. Chapter Performance Objectives

    At the conclusion of this chapter, students should be able to

    a. describe Japan's cultural characteristics and dimensions in terms of the wet garden metaphor

    b. apply their understanding of Japanese values embodied in the wet garden to improve professional and personal relationships with members of the Japanese culture

    c. describe the values defined by the Japanese concepts of *wa* and *shikata (kata)*, *amae*, *seishin*, and *kaizen*, as well as *tatemae* and *honne*.

■ DISCUSSION OF THE CULTURE

1. Description of the Metaphor

   Key Points to Cover

   a. The Japanese garden consists of three basic elements: water (usually a pond with a waterfall), stones, and plants.

   b. Objects for the garden are chosen based on their unique rather than ideal embodiment of the nature of their form, that is, a stone is picked because it has very unique characteristics that are inherent to stones, not because its surface is flawlessly beautiful.

   c. The garden is carefully designed to look natural and artless rather than composed along the lines of the gardener's aesthetic values. The gardener tries hard to select and place items objectively in a way that is harmonious with their nature rather than according to their own sense of order or beauty.

   d. Consideration is given to the passage of time and the effects of season in the garden's appearance. It is designed to reflect the beauty of all of the seasons.

   e. The Japanese spend a significant amount of leisure time meditating in their gardens and contemplating the quiet events of nature (e.g., snow-gazing or moon-watching), which reflects their feeling of harmony and oneness with nature.

   Questions for Discussion

   a. How well does the garden work as a metaphor for the Japanese culture?

   b. Compare the art forms of the Japanese garden and the German symphony. Relate the similarities to shared cultural traits and relate differences to cultural traits that are unique to one of the two cultures.

2. The Country's History and Current Economic Political Situation

   Key Points to Cover

   a. The Japanese are a fairly ancient people who have become very homogeneous. For 11,000 years, up until 1858, they were geographically isolated from outsiders because the previous Ice Age submerged the land bridge connecting the Japanese islands to the rest of Asia. The age and timeless quality of their culture is reflected in the unchanging form of water.

   b. The lack of natural resources in Japan and the resulting Japanese dependence on agriculture and fishing for their existence have resulted in a passionate love of nature, specifically water (rainfall and the sea), which is manifested in the Japanese garden.

   c. Like flowing water that is constantly moving and changing its shape, Japan has weathered enormous political and economic change in the past 125 years, including its industrialization and its utter defeat in a world war.

d. The Japanese concepts of harmony and the value of the group over the individual, which are embodied in the wet garden, were first included in Japanese political values in a 7th-century constitution. This is in contrast to the much newer American political values of the individual rights of life, liberty, and the pursuit of happiness.

e. The Japanese appreciation of beauty led them to study and integrate the foreign artistic, technological, and linguistic accomplishments of the Chinese into their culture as early as the 6th century.

f. The Shogun system of feudalism reinforced the Japanese subjugation of individual needs and talents to the common good of the group, and the shoguns' absolute power over the people engendered the Japanese need to always appear to be behaving correctly or to save face.

Questions for Discussion

a. How have the Japanese dealt with the humiliation of their defeat in World War II? Explain the appropriateness of their actions and feelings in the postwar era using the garden metaphor.

b. Use the metaphor to illustrate how the Japanese borrow Western technological, political, and economic systems and styles freely without undermining their cultural identity.

3. Cultural Dimensions

Key Points to Cover

a. Cultural characteristics

(1) Perception of the individual

(a) The Japanese believe that it takes a great deal of self-discipline to achieve harmony with the natural world, but that individuals have the potential to achieve this harmony through self-mastery and discipline of the spirit, or *seishin*. This value is represented in the painstaking discipline with which the Japanese gardener continually seeks to improve the garden's natural beauty. It is likewise represented in the Japanese virtue of *kaizen* in the workplace, which has evolved into the concept of total quality management. Many Westerners have also come to understand this self-discipline in the form of martial arts training.

(b) The Japanese tend to "flow with the current" over and around small obstacles or differences in opinion, which makes them more tolerant of other viewpoints and gives them a more relative, less rational view of right and wrong. The Japanese view physical pleasures such as sex and drunkenness as natural enjoyments and therefore encourage their enjoyment rather than subjecting them to a code of moral restrictions.

(2) Perception of the world: The Japanese concept of *wa* means to live in harmony with the natural world. The way to achieve *wa* is by finding and following the natural order, which, in turn, determines how things should be done (*shikata*). The Japanese have constructed an entire set of *kata*, or rules governing the correct way to do very specific tasks, to ensure that they are living life in a way that promotes *wa*. Be certain that students understand that *kata* comes from an overriding desire for harmony; the Japanese strict adherence to *kata* can easily be confused with a need to dominate, rather than to live in harmony with the natural world.

(3) Personal relationships: Japanese children are raised to identify themselves more closely with their family and other groups to which they subsequently belong, rather than as an individual with unique desires and ambitions. The value of *amae* is imparted by a child's mother, who rarely leaves the child's side before he or she reaches school age, treats the child as her most valued possession, and is the child's primary source of approval and gratification. *Amae* is illustrated by the power that masses of drops of water possess when they are all traveling in the same direction in a waterfall in a Japanese garden or by a *tsunami* approaching a Japanese fishing village.

(4) Activity: As noted in the sections above, the Japanese believe that they can proactively improve themselves and thereby contribute to the welfare of the group through *kaizen* and by strictly adhering to prescribed *kata*. Therefore, the Japanese are more of a "doing" than a "being" society.

(5) Time

(a) The Japanese perceive time linearly, although the past, present, and future overlap somewhat. This linear conception of time could be tied to the Japanese dependence on agriculture, with its regular progression of seasons, and is illustrated by the unidirectional flow of water.

(b) The Japanese place a slightly greater emphasis on both the present and the future than they do the past, as evidenced by the careful planning of their gardens to take into account future seasons and changes over time.

(6) Space

(a) Japanese houses are not permanently divided into rooms by walls. The space in the house is multifunctional, and furnishings are simple.

(b) Given the design of their houses, privacy is a matter of choice rather than a fact of life, but is generally respected: The Japanese have developed an ability to choose not to hear others' conversations in private situations, such as inside the home. Likewise, in the private space of one's own Japanese garden, great attention and care are given to spatial relationships between objects. However, Japan is a very crowded country, and public space is not at all respected in mass transit or on the streets.

b. Cultural Dimensions of Work Behavior (Hofstede, 1980)

(1) Power distance: Japan scores above the median, higher than the United States but lower than many more autocratic cultures. Although the Japanese use strict hierarchical organizations to preserve the conformity and harmony of the group by carefully defining each member's role, the consensus of the group is highly valued in decision making and implementation.

(2) Uncertainty avoidance: Japan scores very high, higher than almost all of the other nations surveyed by Hofstede.

(a) The Japanese depend on the group, usually their employer in their adult life, for their physical and emotional security. They are not inclined to take risks or deviate from the prescriptions of *kata,* because such actions might result in the group's ineffectiveness or failure.

(b) The Japanese have a very long-range concept of time and are willing to forgo instant gratification for future security.

(3) Individualism: Japan scores below the median and much lower than the Anglo-speaking cluster of countries, but higher than most other Asian societies.

(a) The Japanese tend to be very collectivist and depend on the group for approval and physical security. Therefore, they are much more concerned with the accomplishment of group goals than the pursuit of individual ambitions.

(b) The Japanese appreciation of the individual, however, is higher than in many other Asian cultures, and it is evident in the concept of self-mastery and in the Japanese employment of isolated periods of contemplation in their gardens.

(4) Masculinity: Japan scores very high and is unique from all other countries in its combination of very high masculinity with very high uncertainty avoidance. The Japanese interest in individual self-improvement and good performance is apparently reinforced by their collectivist desire to contribute to the success of the group.

Questions for Discussion

a. How should a foreign visitor to Japan modify his or her behavior in light of the importance of *kata* to the Japanese?

b. Is the concept of honesty defined the same way in Japan as in the United States? Do differences in the concept of honesty mean that the Japanese cannot be depended upon?

c. Are expressions of gratitude expected or appreciated by the Japanese?

d. Current media coverage has emphasized the growing disparity between American and Japanese schoolchildren's performance on standardized tests. Does this disparity reflect cultural differences? How do the Japanese children's higher scores relate to the performance of Japanese adults in the workplace? Are there educational or other areas where American children outperform the Japanese? What impact will the differences between the two cultures in the areas of education and child rearing have on the future economies of the two countries?

    e. How well can an American expatriate expect to be assimilated into Japanese culture and accepted by the Japanese? What steps can he or she take that will contribute the most to the success of his or her assimilation?

4. Religious Values

Key Points to Cover

    a. Zen Buddhism emphasizes self-mastery or *seishin* training as the way to divine the natural order of the cosmos and become one with the universe, and it stresses the importance of ongoing discipline necessary to the art of the Japanese garden.

    b. The indigenous Japanese religion of Shintoism is based on nature worship, which can be seen in the Japanese appreciation of the beauty of nature.

Questions for Discussion

    a. How do the temple architecture and the rituals of Shintoism reflect Japanese cultural values?

    b. How does the Buddhist understanding of the universe shape the Japanese perception of the world, the individual, and personal relationships?

5. Personal Lives and Relationships

Key Points to Cover

    a. Just as the Japanese identify themselves primarily in terms of the groups to which they belong, so, too, are objects in a Japanese garden placed in groups with careful attention to the relationships defined between them.

    b. The Japanese often socialize with members of their groups; the family is the primary and most important social unit, but social relationships with one's colleagues, schoolmates, or fellow volunteer group members are also important and are cultivated with the dedication of a Japanese gardener to the cultivation of his or her plants.

    c. Continual self-improvement and rigid adherence to prescribed codes of conduct are essential to winning the approval of the group.

    d. To preserve the harmony of the group, the Japanese go to great lengths to avoid causing one another embarrassment or shame; therefore, shame is an obvious sign of the group's disapproval and a powerful deterrent to deviant behavior.

Questions for Discussion

    a. Are the Japanese an affectionate people? How do they display affection toward children and among adults?

b. How can the double standard regarding extramarital affairs by men versus women be explained using the metaphor of the garden?

c. What is the students' opinion of the use of shame to control Japanese behavior? Do they agree with the parallel drawn in the chapter between shame and guilt?

d. Explain the dramatic difference in Japanese behavior in public and in private using the values illustrated in the metaphor.

6. Professional Lives and Working Relationships (motivation, leadership decision making, planning accomplishment, communication style, business strengths, and business weaknesses)

Key Points to Cover

a. The Japanese seek individual improvement and achievement to increase their contribution to the welfare of the group, just as the Japanese gardener gives careful attention to every object to perfect the garden as a whole.

b. Japanese leaders are highly respected, hold a great deal of power, and receive many special privileges, but generally, they rely on consensus rather than an authoritarian style of management. Likewise, the Japanese gardener does not try to control the elements of the garden to create beauty as much as he or she tries to bring out their inherent beauty.

c. Deviation from the conformity of the group disturbs its harmony and detracts from its success; therefore, incorrect behavior and self-promotion are discouraged in the same way that objects in a Japanese garden are designed to blend in with rather than stand out from the overall design. The value is embodied in the dual concepts of *tatemae* and *honne,* which are, respectively, the accepted public face and one's personal viewpoint that is subjugated to it.

Questions for Discussion

a. What types of incentives will motivate Japanese workers to work harder? Explain their needs and wants in terms of the garden metaphor.

b. Outside of the office, what should a foreign businessman do to develop a good working relationship with the Japanese?

c. How long does decision making take in Japan? Once a decision is made, will implementation go quickly and smoothly? How reliable are the Japanese in keeping their commitments?

d. How do Japanese prioritize work and leisure time?

e. Which of the typical Japanese employee's attitudes toward work and management would be most different from the students' own?

f. What type of management style will work well for an American manager assigned to a position in Japan? Have the students try to answer the question using management and conflict management models (see Chapter 8).

◼ ACTIVITIES AND EXERCISES

The following activities can be used in any combination to help reinforce the wet garden metaphor for Japanese culture with visual, hands-on, and/or multisensory learning experiences.

1. Role Playing

   Have students act out an ordinary business situation, such as a group project meeting, a job interview, or a performance review. Have at least one student in each group role-play a native for 5 to 10 minutes while others act the way they normally would given the situation. If possible, have each student try playing the Japanese for a short time. At the end of the allotted time, debrief the entire class together, and ask students to comment on those aspects of their assumed role that were the most difficult for them to adjust to. Students will role-play more effectively if the activity takes place after an in-depth discussion of the metaphor (see Exercise 8.6).

2. Tour a Japanese Garden

   Show a videotape demonstrating Japanese gardening techniques, or have the students visit a Japanese garden outside of class. Ask the students to discuss their opinion of the garden's beauty, presentation, and mood. Have them discuss the relationships of the objects to each other and as a part of the garden as a whole, as well as the function of the pond and how it fits into the garden's overall design.

   Viewing a Japanese garden before discussing the metaphor can greatly enhance the students' use of the metaphor elements in the discussion, although the activity is also beneficial if used to reinforce key points afterward. This activity can also be enhanced if a native Japanese gardener can come and speak to the class about the actual techniques used in creating the garden.

3. Case Analysis

   Choose a case that illustrates a cross-cultural problem involving a Japanese worker or organization. Ask the students to complete a case analysis, either as part of their homework assignment or in class groups, using the metaphor to support their conclusions about the contribution of the Japanese cultural traits to the problem. Students' recommendations should be supported by the metaphor as well; for example, if a management strategy conflicted with basic Japanese values, they should show that the new strategy fits into the Japanese value system by referring back to the garden metaphor. The case study should be completed after reading the chapter or after the class discussion.

4. Guest Speakers

   Have a native of Japan, preferably someone involved in management who has had experience in cross-cultural business settings, come and relate his or her experience to the class. If possible, it would be particularly interesting to have a native Japanese guest speaker in conjunction with either the role-playing exercise or the case analysis suggested above, so that he or she could provide accurate critiques of the students' understanding of the Japanese culture.

If it is not possible to arrange for a native Japanese speaker, perhaps an international manager with a great deal of business experience in Japan could be scheduled. This type of speaker may not offer the same depth of insight into the Japanese culture as a native could, but he or she will have a lot of experiences to talk about from the point of view of the foreign manager trying to learn the ropes.

◼ CHAPTER PERFORMANCE REVIEW

1. Students' Review of Their Previous and Current Perceptions of the Culture

   The following questions will help students assess the progress they have made in understanding the Japanese culture through the use of the garden metaphor.

   Questions for Discussion

   a. How accurate were the students' preconceptions of the Japanese culture?

   b. Were there major aspects of the Japanese culture of which the students had been unaware before reading the metaphor chapter?

2. Review the Chapter Performance Objectives

   The following questions will help the instructor evaluate student contribution to class discussion to determine whether or not the chapter objectives have been met.

   a. Were students able to use the garden metaphor in describing Japan's cultural characteristics and dimensions?

   b. Were students able to readily apply their understanding of Japanese values embodied in the garden to either activities simulating interactions with Japanese or hypothetical business situations involving Japanese colleagues?

   c. Can the students define the Japanese concepts of *wa* and *shikata (kata)*, *amae, seishin,* and *kaizen,* as well as *tatemae* and *honne*?

CHAPTER 11

Training Videos and Web Sites

Cross-cultural training videos help to enrich the learning process. My strong preference is for videos containing several short vignettes or incidents lasting 2 to 3 minutes to encourage active learning. Before showing a video, the instructor can present theories and perspectives. After each vignette, the instructor can ask the trainees or students to analyze it in terms of these theories and perspectives, as suggested in several of the exercises in this book. The objective is a discussion or dialogue about the incident.

I have not recommended any feature-length cross-cultural films. There are many such films available that can be obtained easily in the foreign film section of a video store. Such films can be very educational, and the instructor can devote many enjoyable hours to watching them. However, by definition, there is less involvement of the students and trainees in the learning process, because they must sit for about 2 hours before discussing a film, by which time they may have forgotten some of the major issues that were presented.

Given my preferences, I have found only a small number of cross-cultural training videos to be particularly useful. My favorites are as follows:

- *Going International, Part 2: Managing the Overseas Assignment.* About 30 minutes. Copeland Griggs Production, San Francisco. Phone: 415-668-4200. Although somewhat dated, this video includes five excellent cross-cultural incidents involving Americans with Arabs, Asian Indians, Japanese, English, and Mexicans.

- *Work Abroad!* This video was made by Terra Cognita, New York City. Phone: 212-262-4529. It is really an updated version of *Going International, Part 2* and focuses specifically on six themes: communication patterns, individual/group dynamics, time, building relationships, impact of status and hierarchy, and different reasoning processes. I use this video to bring into perspective the theories of Hofstede, Hall, and so on. In so doing, I quickly bypass the captions focusing on the six themes. Otherwise, the instructor is in danger of being too didactic, and the students may become too passive.

■ *Crosstalk at Work: Part 1: Performance Appraising Across Cultures.* About 30 minutes. Available through BBC, Canada. Phone: 416-469-1505. This video includes simulations of actual interviews conducted at the Bank of America. Each goal-setting simulation takes place at the beginning and end of the year, and involves the following female roles, thus eliminating the issue of gender: White American superior and subordinate; White American superior and Chinese American subordinate; and Chinese American superior (who was the subordinate in a preceding role play) and Korean American subordinate. The fact that culture is so important in interactions involving citizens who have lived all or most of their lives in the United States is very instructive. This video is accompanied by an excellent training manual.

■ *West Meets East in Japan,* 37 minutes, available through Intercultural Press, Yarmouth, ME. Phone: 800-370-2665 (USA) or 207-846-5168. The sections on saying no, business cards, and dinners are exemplary.

■ *Cold Water,* 37 minutes. Available through Intercultural Press, as above. Several international students discuss their initial reactions to Americans and how these have changed over time. This is a good introductory training video for students, but not for managers. One surprising reaction among some American students, after watching the entire video, is, If you don't like the U.S., why don't you go home? Typically, these students have had less exposure to cross-cultural ideas and experiences. As a result, the instructor should try to follow the training manual, stopping the video periodically to ask questions and emphasize themes.

■ *Managing in China,* about 40 minutes. Changing Nature of Work, Glenshaw, PA. Phone: 412-487-6639. This video has some technical problems and is slow in parts, but it relates well to the cultural metaphor of the Chinese Family Altar. Perhaps the most compelling part of this video focuses on American-trained Chinese, who comment on their experiences since returning to China, particularly when some of them refuse to show their faces for fear of governmental retribution.

■ *Hell Camp,* about 30 minutes. Films for the Humanities and Sciences, Inc., P.O. Box 2053, Princeton, NJ 08543-2053. Although somewhat dated, this video about a special managerial training program in Japan is striking. It is particularly useful when discussing individualism and collectivism.

■ *The Kyocera Experiment.* MTI Teleprograms, Northbrook, IL 60062. 1-800-323-6301. Although dated, this video does an effective job of describing the activities of work groups in Japan and in the United States, whose members work for the Japanese Kyocera Company. This video fits well with Exercise 4.19, Organization Design and Work Groups.

■ Big World, Inc., in Denver, Colorado makes and distributes an excellent group of nation-specific videos, *Doing Business In . . .* Each video is about 35 minutes long. Phone: 303-444-6179. Typically, each video provides an overview of the nation and its history, economy, etiquette, business relationships, communicating styles, values, negotiating styles, and management. However, it is difficult to use these videos for higher-level concepts such as the cross-cultural dimensions (power distance, uncertainty avoidance, etc.). Also, videos on closely related nations, such as those in Southeast Asia, tend to repeat the same or similar information. Still, these videos are excellent if the instructor is focusing on a specific nation. One major caution is that some of the information tends to become dated rather quickly, such as the political party in power.

In the area of cross-cultural negotiations, the following videos are excellent:

- *Dealing With Conflict,* about 20 minutes. CRM Films. Phone: 1-800-421-0833. Ken Thomas narrates this video highlighting the five styles of negotiating and how they relate to distributive and integrative bargaining. Various incidents or scenarios are used to illustrate these styles.

- *Managers as Mediators.* CorVision, 35 minutes. Phone: 847-537-3130. Buffalo Grove, IL. Mark and Ryan, who are co-workers, have a conflict. Cindy acts as mediator.

- *Negotiating,* about 28 minutes. American Management Association, New York City. This video features a negotiation session between two managers.

- *International Negotiating,* about 30 minutes. Big World, Inc., Boulder, CO. Phone: 303-444-6179. This video provides an excellent overview on negotiation, particularly in the international context.

Finally, there are many Web sites on culture, and several are excellent. These include www.worldculture.com; www.scpworld.com/future/tcoc.htm; www.uark. edu/depts/comminfo/www/intercultural.html; www.june29.com/hlp/; and www. worldculture.com/gestures.htm.

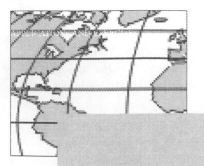

References

Adler, N. (1997). *International dimensions of organizational behavior* (3rd ed.). Boston: South-Western College Publishing.

Brislin, R. (1993). *Understanding culture's influence on behavior.* New York: Harcourt Brace.

Burke, R. (1979). Methods of resolving superior-subordinate conflict. *Organizational Behavior and Human Performance, 5,* 396-410.

Carroll, S., & Gannon, M. (1997). *Ethical dimensions of international management.* Thousand Oaks, CA: Sage.

Chatman, J. A., & Barsade, S. G. (1995). Personality, organizational culture, and cooperation: Evidence from a business simulation. *Administrative Science Quarterly, 40,* 423-443.

Cohen, H. (1982). *You can negotiate anything.* New York: Bantam/Doubleday.

Cottle, T. (1967). The circles test: An investigation of perception of temporal relatedness and dominance. *Journal of Projective Technique and Personality Assessments, 31,* 58-71.

Cox, T. (1993). *Cultural diversity in organizations.* San Francisco: Berrett-Koehler.

Ekman, P., Friesen, W., & Bear, J. (1984, May). The international language of gestures. *Psychology Today,* pp. 64-69.

England, G. (1975). *The manager and his values.* Cambridge, MA: Ballinger.

Fisher, G. (1988). *Mindsets: The role of culture and perception in international relations.* Yarmouth, ME: Intercultural Press.

Fisher, R., Ury, W., & Patton, B. (1991). *Getting to Yes* (rev. ed.). New York: Penguin.

Fiske, A. (1994). *Structures of social life: The four elementary forms of human relations.* New York: Free Press.

Ford, J. (1999). Collecting nos. In R. Lewicki, D. Saunders, & J. Minton (Eds.), *Negotiations: Readings, exercises, and cases* (3rd ed.). New York: Irwin/McGraw-Hill.

France, V. (1999). *An examination of the effectiveness of emotional and informational appeals among Hispanic-Americans in the United States.* Bachelor's degree honors thesis, Department of Psychology, University of Maryland, College Park.

Franke, R., Hofstede, G., & Bond, M. (1991). Cultural roots of economic performance: A research note. *Strategic Management Journal, 12,* 165-173.

Gannon, M. (1988). *Management.* Needham Heights, MA: Allyn & Bacon.

Gannon, M. (1998, June). *Integrating context, cross-cultural dimensions, and cultural metaphors in management education and training.* Paper presented at the Biennial International Conference of the Western Academy of Management, Istanbul, Turkey.

Gannon, M. (Ed.). (2001). *Cultural metaphors: Readings, research translations, and commentary.* Thousand Oaks, CA: Sage.

Gannon, M. J., & Associates. (1994). *Understanding global cultures: Metaphorical journeys through 17 countries.* Thousand Oaks, CA: Sage.

Gannon, M., & Associates. (1997, August). *Cultural metaphors as frames of reference for nations: A six country study.* Paper presented at the annual meeting of the Academy of Management, Boston, MA.

Gannon, M. J., & Associates. (2001). *Understanding global cultures: Metaphorical journeys through 23 countries.* Thousand Oaks, CA: Sage.

Gannon, M., & Audia, P. (in press). The cultural metaphor: A grounded method for analyzing national cultures. In C. Earley & H. Singh (Eds.), *Work behavior across cultures and nations.* Thousand Oaks, CA: Sage.

Hall, E. (1968). *The hidden dimension.* NY: Doubleday.

Hall, E., & Hall, M. (1990). *Understanding cultural differences.* Yarmouth, ME: Intercultural Press.

Hofstede, G. (1980). *Culture's consequences.* Thousand Oaks, CA: Sage.

Hofstede, G. (1991). *Cultures and organizations: Software of the mind.* New York: McGraw-Hill.

Hofstede, G., & Bond, M. (1988). The Confucius connection: From cultural roots to economic growth. *Organizational Dynamics, 16*(4), 4-21.

Kagitcibasi, C. (1990). Family and home-based intervention. In R. Brislin (Ed.), *Applied cross-cultural psychology* (pp. 121-141). Newbury Park, CA: Sage.

Kashima, Y., & Callan, V. (1994). The Japanese work group. In H. Triandis, M. Dunnette, & L. Hough (Eds.), *Handbook of industrial and organizational psychology* (2nd ed., Vol. 4). Palo Alto, CA: Consulting Psychologists Press.

Kluckholn, F., & Strodtbeck, F. (1961). *Variations in value orientations.* Evanston, IL: Row, Peterson.

Lambert, W., Hamers, J., & Frasure-Smith, N. (1979). *Child-rearing values: A cross-national study.* New York: Praeger.

Laurent, A. (1983). The cultural diversity of western conceptions of management. *International Studies of Management and Organization, 12*(1-2). Armonk, NY: Sharpe.

Lewicki, R., Saunders, D., & Minton, J. (Eds.) (1999). Ford, J. (1999). Collecting nos. In *Negotiations: Readings, exercises, and cases* (3rd ed.). New York: Irwin/McGraw-Hill.

Life lesson. (1997, July 9). *Wall Street Journal,* p. A1.

Osland, J., & Bird, A. (2000). Beyond sophisticated stereotyping: Cultural sensemaking in context. *Academy of Management Executive, 14*(1), 65-77.

Pearce, C., & Osmond, C. (1996, Winter). Metaphors for change: The ALPs model of change management. *Organizational Dynamics,* pp. 23-35.

Peng, M. (in press). Strategies, structures, and the state: An institutional analysis. In M. Gannon & K. Newman (Eds.), *Handbook of cross-cultural management.* London: Blackwell.

Phillips, D. (1994, August 21). Building a "culture index" to world airline safety. *Washington Post,* p. A8.

Schein, E. (1985). *Organizational culture and leadership.* San Francisco: Jossey-Bass.

Side by side. (1994, May 3). *Wall Street Journal,* pp. A1, A8.

Simon, H., & Dearborn, D. (1958). Selective perception. *Sociometry, 21,* 140-144.

Smith, H. (1991). The world's religions. San Francisco: Harper.

Smith, K., Grimm, C., & Gannon, M. (1992). *Dynamics of competitive strategy.* Thousand Oaks, CA: Sage.

Smith, P., & Bond, M. (1998). *Social psychology across cultures* (2nd ed.). Boston: Allyn & Bacon.

Smith, P., & Schwartz, S. (1996). Values. In C. Kagitcibasi, M. Segal, & J. Berry (Eds.), *Handbook of cross-cultural psychology* (2nd ed., Vol. 3), pp. 77-118. Boston: Allyn & Bacon.

Thase, M., Frank, E., & Kupfer, D. (1985). Biological processes in major depression. In E. Beckman & W. Leber (Eds.), *Handbook of depression: Treatment, assessment, and research* (pp. 816-913). Homewood, IL: Dorsey.

Tinsley, C. (1998). Models of conflict resolution in Japanese, German, and American cultures. *Journal of Applied Psychology, 83,* 316-323.

Triandis, H. (in press). Generic types of individualism and collectivism. In M. Gannon & K. Newman (Eds.), *Handbook of cross-cultural management.* London: Blackwell.

Trompenaars, F., & Hampden-Turner, C. (1998). *Riding the waves of culture* (2nd ed.). New York: McGraw-Hill.

Weiss, S. (1994, Spring). Negotiating with "Romans"—Part 2. *Sloan Management Review,* pp. 85-100.

Yando, R., Seitz, V., & Zigler, E. (1979). *Intellectual and personality characteristics of children: Social-class and ethnic-group differences.* Hillsdale, NJ: Lawrence Erlbaum.

Index

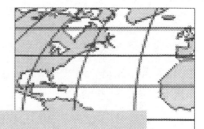

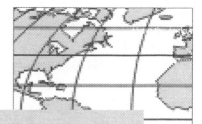

About the Author

Martin J. Gannon (PhD, Columbia University) is Professor of Management and Director of the Center for Global Business, Robert H. Smith School of Business, University of Maryland at College Park. He is also the Founding Director of the College Park Scholars Program in Business, Society, and the Economy (an undergraduate living-learning community). His previous positions at Maryland include Associate Dean for Academic Affairs, Chair of the Faculty of Management and Organization, and Co-Founder/Co-Director of the Small Business Development Center. At Maryland, he teaches in the areas of international management and behavior and business strategy. He is the author or coauthor of 85 articles and 13 books, including *Dynamics of Competitive Strategy* (Sage, 1992); *Understanding Global Cultures: Metaphorical Journeys Through 17 Nations* (Sage, 1994, revised ed., 2001), *Managing Without Traditional Methods: International Innovations in Human Resource Management* (1996); and *Ethical Dimensions of International Management* (Sage, 1997).

Professor Gannon has served as a management consultant and trainer to a large number of private firms, federal government agencies, and labor unions. He has class-tested the applications and exercises in this book with managers, MBA students, and undergraduate students in many nations. Specific organizations for which he has consulted include the Strategic Forum Consulting Group in Malaysia and Indonesia; the Polish-American Center, University of Lodz, Pland; Bocconi University, Milan; Universities of Tübingen and Kassel, Germany; University College–Dublin; London Business School; Universiti Kabangsaan, Malaysia; and Thammasat University, Bangkok. Currently, he is the main external consultant to GEICE Insurance Company on the design and delivery of its Senior Management Training Program. He is University of Maryland Academic Director of the Northrop-Grumman Managerial IMPACT Certificate Program designed to increase international skill sets.

Professor Gannon has been Senior Research Fulbright Professor at the Center for the Study of Work and Higher Education in Germany and the John F. Kennedy/Fulbright Professor at Thammasat University in Bangkok, as well as a visiting professor at several Asian and European universities.

Mark Sperring

Laura Ellen Anderson

SNAPPY
BIRTHDAY

BLOOMSBURY

LONDON NEW DELHI NEW YORK SYDNEY

One day an invitation
came to number 24.
It was from a next door neighbour
who they'd never met before.
It said . . .

COME TO MY
BIRTHDAY PARTY
(it's at number 22).

I really, really, **really**
want to celebrate with you!

So PLEASE just bring your
little selves
(don't bring a thing for me).

The NICEST gift of ALL would be

TO HAVE YOU ALL
FOR
TEA.

There wasn't much to think about –
of course they had to go.
For, who doesn't like a party?
Well . . . nobody I know!

So, they ran up to their bedrooms
and pulled out things to wear,

with stripes and spots
and lots of dots
and ribbons everywhere!

And while they all got ready,
they chatted merrily
about the treats that lay in store
and who their host could be . . .

Yes, who had sent that invite?
And what would they be like?
It must be someone lovely!
(But – hmm – would they be right?)

When they arrived that afternoon
at number 22,
the front door swung right open
and a voice cried out . . . .

And there he stood . . .
their neighbour
(a green and tall-ish chap).
He bowed and said politely,
"Pleased to meet you,
my name's Snap!"

He beckoned to them sweetly,
with a newly sharpened claw,
and said . . .
"Come in my **cherry plums**.
Don't linger at the door!"

Once ushered in the children
did their best to be polite.
But a crocodile-birthday-boy
was quite a SHOCKING sight!

Snap smiled, "Don't look so worried.
We'll have fun without a doubt.
Now how about a party game?"
Then . . .

They ran till they grew tired –
till their little legs grew weak.

Cried Snap,
"I cannot find you!

Are we playing
hide and seek?"

He hunted high and hunted low.
Oh, what a thrilling game!
Then suddenly, he found them –

Boo!

– which was an awful shame . . .

For Snap led them to his table
where there sat one single plate.
And, when the clock struck teatime,
said, "I think it's time I ate!"

He told those dear, sweet children,
"Yes, it's YOU I'm
going to eat.
For nothing could taste nicer –
you're the perfect birthday treat!"

"But, Snap!"
their little voices cried,
"How very wrong you are.
On special days like birthdays
there's a nicer treat by far!"

And suddenly the room went dark,
Snap heard a birthday cheer.

"Hip, hip,

"hooray!"

the children cried.

"We've brought you something – here!"

And almost out of thin air,
came a cake all pink and green.
With chocolate drops and candy hearts –

the
BIGGEST
cake you've ever seen!

Snap gulped it down in one great gulp! And –

YUM!

– who would have guessed?
That on special days like birthdays,
children really **don't** taste best!

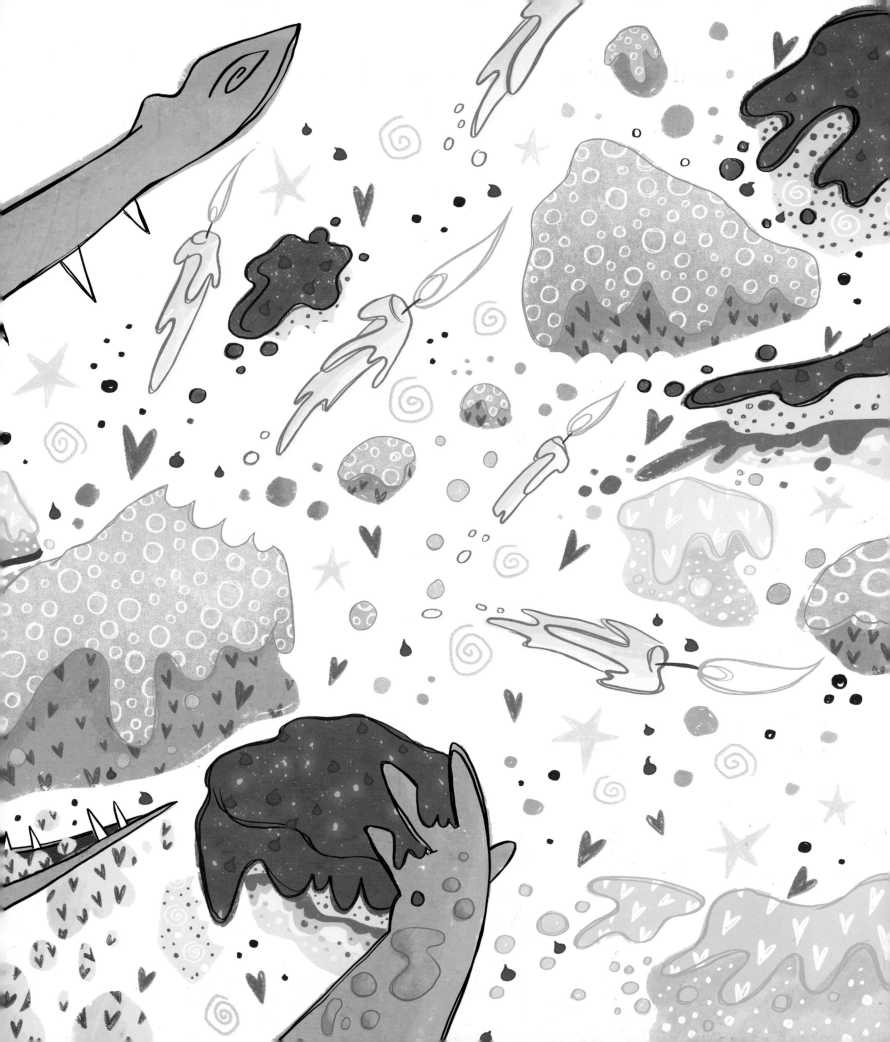

Snap licked his lips and thanked them,
"What a lovely thing to bring!
Yes, it's been fun, now off you run.
I couldn't eat another thing."

For Sarah my Doodle-Muse! – MS

For my Great Grandad Tommy,
who always believed in me and helped me
to achieve my dreams. You will always
have a special place in my heart – LEA

Bloomsbury Publishing, London, New Delhi, New York and Sydney

First Published in Great Britain in 2015 by Bloomsbury Publishing Plc
50 Bedford Square, London, WC1B 3DP

Text copyright © Mark Sperring 2015
Illustrations copyright © Laura Ellen Anderson 2015
The moral rights of the author and illustrator have been asserted

A CIP catalogue record of this book is available from the British Library

ISBN 978 1 4088 5261 3 (HB)
ISBN 978 1 4088 5262 0 (PB)
ISBN 978 1 4088 5260 6 (eBook)

Printed in China by Leo Paper Products, Heshan, Guangdong

1 3 5 7 9 10 8 6 4 2

All papers used by Bloomsbury Publishing are natural, recyclable products made
from wood grown in well-managed forests. The manufacturing processes
conform to the environmental regulations of the country of origin

www.bloomsbury.com

BLOOMSBURY is a registered trademark of Bloomsbury Publishing Plc